NADIA BOULANGER

NADIA BOULANGER

by

Jérôme Spycket

"Enthusiasm and order"
Paul Valéry

English translation by M. M. Shriver

PENDRAGON PRESS
STUYVESANT NY

Other Biographical Titles from Pendragon Press

Liszt, Caroline, and the Vatican Documents by Alan Walker with Gabriele Erasmi (1991) ISBN 0-945193-09-2

Archduke Rudolf, Beethoven's Patron, Pupil, and Friend: His Life and Music by Susan Kagan (1989) ISBN 0-918728-74-6

The Letters of Fanny Hensel to Felix Mendelssohn collected, edited, and translated with introductory essays and notes by Marcia J. Citron (1986) ISBN 0-918728-52-5

The Many Lives of Otto Kahn by Mary Jane Matz (1984) ISBN 0-918728-36-3

Schoenberg Remembered by Dika Newlin (1980) ISBN 0-918728-14-2

The original French edition of this book was published in 1987 by Editions Payot Lausanne for the centennial of the birth of Nadia Boulanger

Printed in the United States of America

In Memory of Sylvie

Library of Congress Cataloging-in-Publication Data

Spycket, Jérôme.
    [Nadia Boulanger. English]
    Nadia Boulanger / by Jérôme Spycket ; English translation by M.M. Shriver
      p. cm.
    Includes bibliographical references and index.
    ISBN 0-945193-38-6 :
    1. Boulanger, Nadia. 2. Music teachers--France--Biography.
I. Title.
ML423.B52S713   1992
780'.92--dc20
[B]
                                           92-25835
                                              CIP
                                              MN

Contents

Nadia Boulanger (1887–1979)

Foreword

Il y a des noms qui échappent au cyclone de l'indifférence, à l'ogre de l'actualité: le nom de Nadia Boulanger en est le type car il se place à un point do noblesse qui le rend invisible au médiocre.

Jean Cocteau, 1957

This work is not a biography: certain biographical details are still shrouded in darkness and may perhaps be illumined when documents entrusted to the Bibliothèque Nationale and not to be opened until 2009, become accessible. This book is simply an attempt to recall vividly to mind, through the medium of a few key actors or events in her life-story, the legendary personage, born just over a hundred years ago, that was Nadia Boulanger.

Venerated, feared or opposed, she was as famous the world over as the most prestigious of performers, or the best known of composers. Although she was herself both a performer and a composer, it was not in those capacities that she won world renown: she owed her fame to her knowledge of music, and to her genius for transmitting that knowledge. "Living in the realm of music is such a source of joy to me that I was determined to share it in my teaching with all the means in my power," she declared toward the end of her life. For the first three-quarters of this century, countless young musicians crowded around her piano where, with rigor and passion, she opened up to them a universe hitherto unknown.

But behind this somewhat formal and mythical personality was there not another, hidden by an excessive reserve? I would like to add a personal touch here: personal but certainly not unique.

I had the privilege of taking part in a few concerts under the direction of Nadia Boulanger. Very young singer that I was, I lived in a constant agony of fear that I might fail to measure up to her demanding musical standards. However, on the occasion of my very first rehearsal, that did not keep me from opposing her vigorously with all the brashness of youth on a strictly vocal point. For a moment she seemed completely taken aback, but she did not insist, and she never brought the matter up again. And, some time later, her behavior showed clearly that she held no grudge against me for having stood up to her.

This happened at the beginning of August, 1959, at Gstaad, when the Menuhin Festival was taking place. After a morning rehearsal in Yehudi Menuhin's chalet, "Nadia" decided to go for a walk, and she asked me if I would like to go along.

We set off at a good pace through the Swiss mountain pastureland in the soft blue-tinted light of a radiant summer day. ("Delightful weather. A slight mist," she jotted down in her little notebook.) I realize now that she was then almost seventy-two years old—impossible to believe, so boundless was her vitality, energy, and enthusiasm.

When we were about to retrace our steps, she stopped on the verge of a meadow: I can still see her clearly in my mind's eye, standing there dressed in a short-sleeved white shirtwaist and a severe gray skirt that came almost to her ankles (drawing attention to her sturdy black walking shoes).

She leaned against a wooden gate, and suddenly a metamorphosis took place: the legendary personage, all rigor and conviction, fascinating but sometimes stern to the point of harshness, had relaxed her guard, revealing a glimpse of another woman, or rather of the woman beneath the public figure, so human and obviously vulnerable that I was dumbfounded. Her tone softened; she spoke more slowly, the note of authority completely vanished from her voice. The conversation was by no means intimate, but the distance between us had been erased.

Even though I cannot remember word for word what she said, I shall never forget the sweetness of her smile. It was not a smile of the lips only; her beautiful face, soft-framed in gray hair, shone with an expression of great tenderness.

This privileged interlude lasted ten minutes at the most, and I never experienced another like it, but the great sensitivity I had seen in her lives on; a strange, deeply moving, marvelous memory.

And it is this rare image of Nadia Boulanger that I would like to suggest the reader glimpse between the lines of the austere life story of this great priestess passionately dedicated to music. For my part, even thirty years later, I cannot think of this special moment without finding myself once again incredulous, spellbound.

Besides, this image of "Nadia" serves only to reinforce, in counterpoint, the profound impression I was left with when I concluded the research necessary for writing this book—an immense admiration, almost awe, for one so like a grand-scale heroine of antiquity, Mademoiselle Boulanger.

J. S. 1987

"Naaadia, Naaadia . . ."

From early childhood right until her end, the imperious call, "Naaadia, Naaadia," repeated in a deep voice laden with the mystery of the Slavic soul, accompanied each moment in the life of "Mademoiselle" Boulanger.

Even after the death of her omnipresent mother, this call, implicit in which was the command to disciplined obedience, followed Nadia throughout her lifetime, ever vivid in her memory, until the day of her own death.

"*Maman* has always been my judge," Nadia Boulanger was wont to say; even when well advanced in years, she did not hesitate to confess, "Mother is still with me; I feel her presence. Time has not changed that."

Who was this mother who left so indelible a mark? Raïssa Mychetsky was a Russian; she claimed to be a princess. Perhaps she really was, though this has never been substantiated. Princess indeed she was, in any case, for her daughter Nadia, who doubtless owed to this real or imagined heredity a love of all that is aristocratic, and a constant need to maintain great dignity of bearing.

A halo of mystery surrounds Raïssa's background and the first nineteen years of her life, which were apparently spent in Saint Petersburg: she was born there on December 19, 1858 (the official date, although certain Russian documents show 1856), and it was in Saint Petersburg that she met Ernest Boulanger, probably in 1874, when he was directing concerts there. She was sixteen, studying voice. Apparently she was deeply smitten with the French musician, forty-three years her senior (he was born in Paris September 16, 1815, and was fifty-nine years old at the time).

Since he was a professor of voice at the Paris Conservatoire, she arranged to join him there, became one of his students, and eventually married him. The marriage took place on September 14, 1877, in Saint Petersburg. The newlyweds left immediately for Paris, where they settled down at 35 rue de Maubeuge.

The "young bridegroom" was sixty-two years old, and was held in high esteem. As the son of the well-known opera singer Marie-Julie Hallinger who had enjoyed a brilliant career at the Opéra-Comique, and the nephew of the famous actor Frédérick Lemaître, Boulanger was involved from his earliest years in the artistic life of the

Raïssa Mychetsky, Ernest Boulanger

capital. Pianist and composer, as a student at the Conservatoire he had won the Prix de Rome when he was nineteen. He went on to compose many light works—including ten or so opéras-comiques—which were much in vogue among his contemporaries.

He had started out as a pianist (in this capacity he made a successful tour in the United States in 1851–1852), then became a conductor before teaching voice at the Conservatoire. He counted among his friends Gounod, Massenet, Saint-Saëns, Ambroise Thomas, as well as Jules Barbier, Jules Verne, critics, performers, painters. . . .

Gounod, after the premiere of *Faust*, which was at first not well received, wrote to inquire of Ernest Boulanger: "Did you really find the dissonances of the Prelude intolerable?"

Raïssa seemed to feel immediately at home in this environment which she must have found completely satisfying. The couple appears to have been happy, but oddly enough for more than seven years the marriage was childless; finally in 1885 on January 16 a daughter was born to them—Nina Juliette, who died the following year.

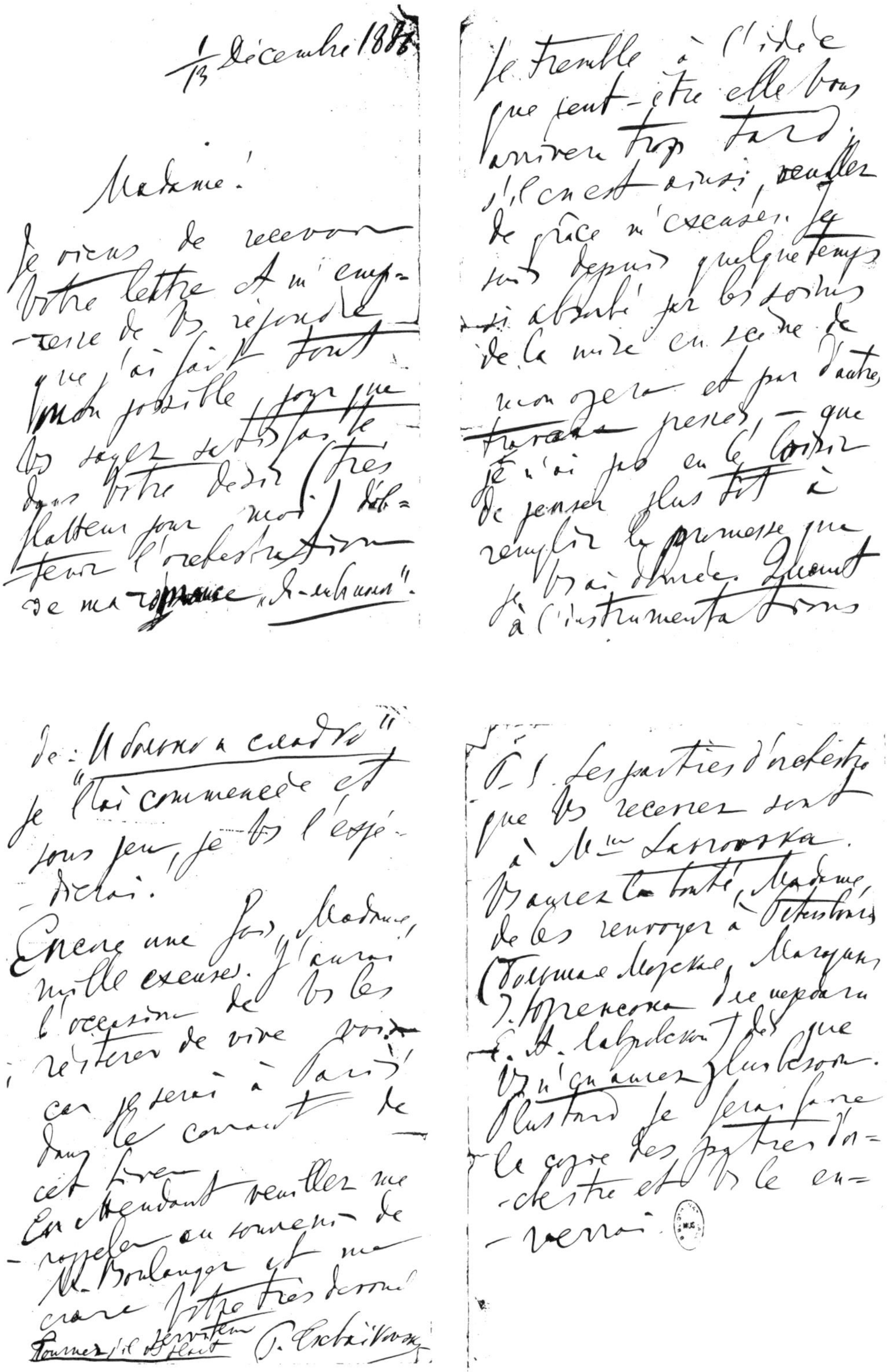
1/13 Décembre 1888

Madame!

Je viens de recevoir votre lettre et m'empresse de vous répondre que j'ai fait tout mon possible pour que vous soyez satisfaite dans votre désir (très flatteur pour moi) d'obtenir l'orchestration de ma romance «Я-ли в поле».

Je tremble à l'idée que peut-être elle vous arrivera trop tard; s'il en est ainsi, veuillez de grâce m'excuser. Je suis depuis quelque temps si absorbé par les soins de la mise en scène de mon opéra et par d'autres travaux pressés, — que je n'ai pas eu le loisir de penser plus tôt à remplir la promesse que je vous ai donnée. Quant à l'instrumentation vous

de: «И больно и сладко» je l'ai commencée et sous peu, je vous l'expédierai.

Encore une fois, Madame, mille excuses. J'aurai l'occasion de vous les réitérer de vive voix car je serai à Paris dans le courant de cet hiver. En attendant veuillez me rappeler au souvenir de M. Boulanger et me croire votre très dévoué serviteur

P. Tchaïkovsky

Tournez s'il vous plaît

P.S. Les parties d'orchestre que vous recevrez sont à Mme Lavrovska. Vous aurez la bonté, Madame, de les renvoyer à Pétersbourg (Большая Морская, Магазин [illegible] для передачи Е. А. Лавровской) dès que vous n'en aurez plus besoin. Plus tard je ferai faire la copie des parties d'orchestre et vous le enverrai.

Letter from Tchaikovsky to Raïssa Boulanger

Was it in an effort to erase the memory of this tragedy that Raïssa went back to her music, or had she perhaps not yet given it up? A letter Tchaikovsky wrote to her in December, 1886, makes one wonder:

> Madame!
>
> I just received your letter and want to let you know right away that I've done everything I can to see that you get what you want (I was very flattered by the request!)—the orchestration of my romance, "Ja li v pole" ("When I was in the field").
>
> I'm very much afraid that it may not get to you in time; if that should be the case, please forgive me. For quite a while I have been so preoccupied with the staging of my opera, and with taking care of other pressing tasks, that this is the first chance I have had to think about keeping my promise to you. As for the instrumentation for "I bolno i sladko" ("Sad and sweet"), I have started on it and will send it to you soon.
>
> Once again, Madame, my sincere apologies. I will have the opportunity to repeat them in person, since I will be in Paris some time this winter.
>
> Meanwhile, please give my best to Monsieur Boulanger, and know that I remain
>
> Your very devoted
P. Tchaikovsky
>
> Please turn the page
>
> P.S. The orchestra parts that are being sent to you belong to Madame Lavrovska. As soon as you are through with them, please return them to Petersbourg (Bol'saja Morskaja, Magazin, G. Jurgenson, to be forwarded to E. A. Lavrovska). I will have the orchestra parts copied out for you and will send them to you later on.

One year later, however, Raïssa was wholly absorbed in caring for her new baby: on September 16, 1887, the very day of Ernest Boulanger's own birthday (his seventy-second), he registered at the Town Hall of the ninth arrondissement of Paris the birth of Juliette Nadia; Jules Barbier and a tradesman by the name of Drouelle signed as witnesses.

From the very first day, Raïssa kept Nadia in her own room. This cohabitation lasted virtually to the day of Madame Boulanger's death, forty-eight years later.

This was only one aspect of Raïssa's astonishing domination of her daughter. Yet, robustly healthy, little Nadia grew up without problems. That is, except for one peculiarity—she was totally, viscerally, allergic to music! The instant she heard a note, she would burst into tears and fly to the farthest corner of the apartment! A curious rejection on the part of a child, who, when she grew up, would declare, "Notes speak faster than words to me: my mind grasps the associations of letters more slowly than it does the associations of notes. I read a written text more hesitantly than I read a score."

Nadia, at one year;

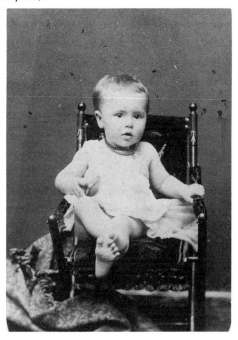

at three . . .;   at six

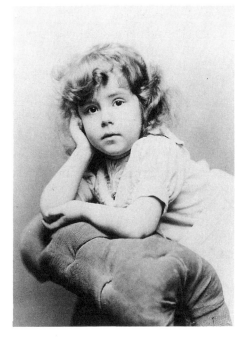

13

Nadia and Lili in April, 1900, on the balcony
of the apartment on the rue La Bruyère

With Gabriel Fauré in 1904

According to Nadia, it was the sound of a fire-engine siren that triggered the initial breakthrough: she was then almost five years old, and her mother was expecting another baby. Marie Juliette was born on the twenty-fourth of August, 1893, in the Boulangers' new apartment, 30 rue La Bruyère, on the edge of the artists' quarter of *la Nouvelle-Athènes*.

Unlike her big sister, Lili—as Marie Juliette was always called—was a delicate child (at three, she had her first attack of pneumonia), but her fragile health did not keep Raïssa from leaving the baby in the care of Ernest Boulanger and a servant in the autumn of 1894, to set off with little Nadia on a trip to Russia and Finland to visit family and friends she had not seen for seventeen years.

When they came back, they found Ernest Boulanger ill, suffering from chronic bronchitis. In January, 1895, he retired from the Conservatoire; this gave him an opportunity to supervise Nadia's first musical studies. At the end of the following year, when she was nine, he enrolled her in a class of solfège at the Conservatoire, and at the same time entrusted her to young Louis Vierne for organ and composition.

Under the iron rod of Madame Boulanger, who kept the whole household whipped into shape, Nadia applied herself diligently. Although she showed no special aptitude, she worked with a conscientiousness and dedication unusual in a child of ten. Little Lili looked on with admiration. As early as 1897, Nadia was rewarded with a First Prize in solfège.

But day after day her mother continued to ram home the lesson: Nadia must never be satisfied with her own progress. No matter how outstandingly well the child did, Raïssa never stopped asking, "Are you quite sure that you couldn't have done better?" Paul Valéry's daughter, Agathe Rouart, a close friend of Nadia's, wrote in her recollections: "In that tone of voice which was more than imperious, she drummed into her daughters total dedication to work. She was far less eager to applaud their success than to demand to know if they had done EVERYTHING they could possibly have done. . ."

On March 24, 1898, Raïssa Boulanger gave birth to another daughter, Léa Marie-Louise. Raïssa was almost forty, and her husband was eighty-two: perhaps that had something to do with the fact that the infant lived less than five months. The birth had been registered once again in the presence of Emile Drouelle, with one of the closest friends of the Boulangers, William Bouwens van den Boijen serving as the other witness. Bouwens and his family were to play an important role in Nadia's life. When Ernest Boulanger died suddenly on April 14, 1900, William Bouwens, Nadia's godfather, was appointed guardian of the Boulanger girls, in accordance with their father's wishes. The two families continued to be very close, and Nadia always thought of the Bouwens children as her brothers and sisters.

Nadia was twelve when her father died; Lili was six. At forty-two, Raïssa became the sole head of the manless household. By the force of circumstances, and with the help of her temperament, she assumed a position of undisputed authority from which her daughter had no recourse. They submitted with remarkable docility.

Their daily life went on as before. In the fall of 1898, Nadia was enrolled in the class in harmony taught by Auguste Chapuis at the Conservatoire. The following May, she took her first communion at Trinity Church. From that point onward, she often manifested a proselytizing zeal; its deep sincerity was one of Nadia's basic traits, though some people may have criticized certain outward displays of faith as artificial. There is no doubt, however, that Nadia Boulanger, throughout her life, and especially in her last years, found in religion a source of unusual spiritual strength which her own temperament predisposed her to cultivate.

Did she really suffer at the death of Ernest Boulanger, who was old enough to have been her great-grandfather? No doubt she did, but just as one would at the disappearance of any beloved elderly relative.

Nor is there any doubt that the death of her father stepped up the pace of her studies: in the absence of the head of the family, Ernest Boulanger's widow—accustomed to a certain standard of living—faced problems she was not in a position to solve single-handed. Very likely the Bouwenses helped her, but it was up to Nadia to take over as soon as she possibly could. The new responsibilities which her mother had her take on certainly explain Nadia's precocious maturity, her acceptance of rigid discipline, and that indispensable authoritarian manner which so often seemed excessive. Yet she would say towards the end of her life: "When I started out at the Conservatoire, I was very shy. I don't show it any more, but I still am . . ."

The dates that mark Nadia's swift progress bear eloquent witness to the efforts she made, despite her tender years. She was only thirteen in the fall of 1900 when she enrolled in Paul Vidal's class in accompaniment. In 1901, she was in Gabriel Fauré's class in composition. He took Nadia under his protective wing (in 1903, when she was only sixteen, he had sufficient confidence in her ability to have her serve as his substitute organist at the Madeleine). She found his teaching inspiring. Looking back many years later, she would recall, "During his classes, I never heard him speak about his own music."

At the end of 1901, Nadia was awarded a Second Prize in harmony, and when classes began again in the fall of 1902, she studied organ with Alexandre Guilmant. At this time, her circle of acquaintances included Koechlin, Enesco, Florent Schmitt, Ravel, Cortot, Roger Ducasse (who, until his death in 1954, remained one of her closest friends, as a rich and voluminous exchange of letters between them attests). Nadia's dedication, her infinite capacity for work had already begun to command the admiration of her fellow-students.

She still found time for Lili, who was beginning to "take a stroll through music," without yet knowing that she would devote the whole of her brief life to it: in any case, her health was so delicate that it was out of the question for her to take regular classes.

Lili was almost ten years old when, in 1903, Nadia obtained her First Prize in harmony, prelude to the fireworks which in the following year first drew attention to her excellence: in July, 1904, at sixteen, Nadia carried off, one after the other, a First Prize in organ, in piano accompaniment, in fugue, and in composition.

A few days earlier she had played the organ on the occasion of the primary class presentation (la Fête de l'enseignement primaire) at the Trocadero Palace in the presence of the President of the Republic, Emile Loubet, and side by side with artists of distinction like Marguerite Moreno of the Comédie Française. Madame Boulanger took good care to preserve the program; on its margin she jotted the note: "1st money Nadia has earned"!

From that point onward Nadia never stopped earning: modest sums at first, but brought in fast enough to make an ever increasing contribution toward keeping up the standard of living which her mother had maintained (one wonders how) after her husband's death.

In October, 1904, after spending the summer as they had often spent it in the past at Trouville, Madame Boulanger and her daughters left their apartment in the rue La Bruyère—where Ernest Boulanger's room had been closed up since his death—to move into fifth-floor quarters at 36 rue Ballu on the corner of rue Vintimille. Their new apartment was spacious, but Madame Boulanger still insisted that her daughters continue to share her bedroom. From 1905 on, however, Lili, because of her delicate health and insomnia, was allowed to have a room of her own at the end of the hallway overlooking the courtyard.

Was it just by chance that this new apartment was only two steps away from that of the famous pianist Raoul Pugno, 60 rue de Clichy? All we know for certain is that in the course of her studies at the Conservatoire Nadia had come in contact with Pugno, that he had followed her performance in the competitive examinations with interest, and that a bond had been established between them.

Costume party at Raoul Pugno's home in Hanneucourt: Pugno, standing, left; Nadia, dressed in Alsatian costume is standing behind Lili.

So, when the Cavaillé-Coll organ built for Nadia was installed in the rue Ballu apartment, it was unthinkable that Pugno not be present for its inauguration. He had to decline the first date proposed for this event, declaring with regret, "I would really have very much enjoyed faltering my way through a spur-of-the-moment something!" No matter! Another date was selected at his convenience: February 4, 1905. For this occasion, the invitation cards were gilt-edged!

Madame ERNEST BOULANGER et
Mademoiselle NADIA BOULANGER vous
prient d'assister à l'**Inauguration** de leur
orgue *Mutin-Cavaillé-Coll*, qui aura lieu
le *4* février 1905, à 9 heures très précises.

Y PRENDRONT PART :

Madame A. VIERNE-TASKIN

et Mrs. *Alex. Guilmant. Raoul Pugno Louis Vierne*

R. S. V. P.   *36, rue Ballu*

(Madame Ernest Boulanger and Mademoiselle Nadia Boulanger request the pleasure of your company at the Inauguration of their Mutin-Cavaillé-Coll organ, which will take place on the fourth of February, 1905, promptly at nine o'clock. Taking part will be: Madame A. Vierne-Taskin and Messieurs Alex Guilmant, Raoul Pugno, and Louis Vierne.)

The program was copious, and it is possible that Pugno, besides contributing his improvisations, may have interpreted works for the organ recently composed by Nadia. (See opposite.)

From then on, Raoul Pugno began to play an increasingly important role in Nadia Boulanger's life—or perhaps it may have been the other way around. Beginning in 1905, Madame Boulanger rented a summer home at Hanneucourt, a little town close to Gargenville, near Mantes, where Pugno had a summer retreat, La Maison Blanche: here at Gargenville the Boulangers and Pugno became summertime neighbors, just as they were wintertime neighbors in Paris. And in 1908 Madame Boulanger purchased Les Maisonnettes, a stone's throw away from Pugno's Maison Blanche. And thus, until 1914, their summers were shared, and made pleasant by the festive parties Pugno was fond of giving: he was a man who enjoyed life immensely, loving the company of his friends, among whom were Ysaÿe, Jacques Thibaud, Louis Vierne, Paul Vidal, Mengelberg, and also D'Annunzio or Verhaeren. . .

18

PROGRAMME

1. *Pièce Héroïque*.. .. .. César FRANCK.
Nadia BOULANGER.

2. *Air de la Passion selon St-Jean* . J.-S. BACH.
M. DAVID-DEVRIÈS.

3. *Fantaisie et Fugue* en sol mineur J.-S. BACH.
M. Louis VIERNE.

4. *Air de Rynaldo*. .. .. G.-F. HANDEL.
Mme VIERNE-TASKIN.

5. *Pièces*. .. .. XXX...
M. Raoul PUGNO.

6. *Aria et Final* .. .. G.-F. HANDEL.
Nadia BOULANGER.

7. *Duo du Magnificat* .. .. .. J.-S. BACH.
Mme VIERNE-TASQUIN.
M. DAVID-DEVRIÈS.

8. *Concerto* en ré mineur .. .. G.-F. HANDEL.
I. *Andante quasi allegretto*. — II. *Adagio*. — III. *Allegro*.
M. Alexandre GUILMANT.

9. *Pièces*. .. .. XXX...
M. Raoul PUGNO.

10. *L'Esclave*.. .. .. Edouard LALO.
Mme VIERNE-TASKIN.

11. *Pastorale* .. .. César FRANCK.
M. Louis VIERNE.

12. *Pièces*. .. .. XXX...
M. Raoul PUGNO.

13. *Air des Saisons* . .. . HAYDN.
M. DAVID-DEVRIÈS.

14. a/ *Canon en si majeur* .. .. Robert SCHUMANN.
b/ *Hosannah !* .. .. J. LEMMENS.
M. Alexandre GUILMANT.

Meanwhile, Nadia's career was off and running full tilt, with banners flying. Once settled in the rue Ballu apartment, and fortified by her battery of diplomas, she began giving lessons. When school started up again in the fall of 1905, Nadia—who had just turned eighteen—sounded her rallying call, as she would continue to do year after year, by formally announcing the resumption of her classes:

Mademoiselle Nadia BOULANGER reprendra le 15 Octobre ses leçons particulières de piano, orgue, harmonie, fugue et accompagnement, et recevra le Vendredi de 1 heure à 3 heures.

COURS D'HARMONIE
Inspecté par M. Auguste CHAPUIS
Professeur au Conservatoire.

Du 1ᵉʳ Novembre au 30 Juin

PRIX DES COURS :
Quatre cours par mois . . 30 fr.

COURS DE DÉCHIFFRAGE
à 2 mains, 4 mains, 2 pianos
PRIX DES COURS :
Quatre cours par mois . . 20 fr.

COURS D'ACCOMPAGNEMENT
PIANO & VIOLON
PRIX DES COURS :
Deux cours par mois . . . 20 fr.
Quatre cours par mois . . 30 fr.

Mademoiselle BOULANGER admet dans ces cours les pianistes qui ne suivent pas son enseignement, mais désirent faire de la musique d'ensemble.

36, Rue Ballu.

At the Pugno's in Hanneucourt around 1910. Raoul Pugno, top center; immediately to his left, Madame Boulanger; Nadia, lower at the extreme left; Lili in the middle of the second row; leaning toward her, Magda Tagliaferro.

In residence at Compiègne in 1907 for the Prix de Rome

This was the start of her famous group lessons. Later these classes would take place on Wednesdays, always followed by a session around the samovar, presided over by Madame Boulanger, who served tea and little cakes to her daughter's pupils. Even after Madame Boulanger's death this rite continued to be faithfully observed until World War II.

Pugno (like Fauré, Vierne, and others) sent pupils to Nadia. It was thanks to Pugno's recommendation that Nadia acquired her first American students, who in turn gave her lessons in English.

But hand in hand with her teaching, Nadia Boulanger plunged into a performing career: now at the organ, now at the piano, sometimes as soloist, sometimes as accompanist, she began to perform on a regular basis in Paris. Here too Pugno's support was significant, and in 1906 they even began to give concerts together.

This collaboration became increasingly closer knit, branching out to include composing together. Quite possibly it was at Pugno's urging that Nadia presented herself as a candidate in the Concours de Rome, from which no woman had as yet carried off the First Prize in music. Two attempts, in 1906 and 1907, were not successful for Nadia. To compensate for this disappointment, Pugno invited her to spend part of the summer of 1907 at his property in Saint-Jean-Cap-Ferrat.

In May, 1908, Nadia returned once again to Compiègne for the Prix de Rome competition: of the ten candidates, she was the youngest, and the only woman. She proceeded to stir up a storm of controversy: she composed the mandatory fugue assigned to the semi-finalists for string quartet rather than for singers. Some members of the jury, including Saint-Saëns, demanded that she be disqualified for this infraction of the rules, but thanks to her champions (Pugno?), the matter was referred to the Académie des Beaux-Arts, who decided in her favor, and authorized her to participate in the finals along with the remaining five candidates (among whom was Philippe Gaubert).

Without any doubt, no matter how excellent her cantata, *Sirène*, may have been, this incident—coupled with the fact that she was a woman—removed any hope she might have had of obtaining the First Grand Prize. And indeed she had to settle for second place. Yet she made an attempt to smooth Saint-Saëns' ruffled feathers by writing him a letter in which she explained her reasons for doing what she had done, and assuring him that she had not been motivated by any desire "to draw attention to myself by deliberately going out of my way to appear original."

By return mail, Saint-Saëns sent her an answer from London, dated May 10, 1908:

Mademoiselle,

It is clear: if you wrote your fugue for two violins, viola and bass, and if you brought along four instrumentalists to perform it, it was what everyone was doing!

Despite the fact that you have spent several years in composition class, and that this is not your first time in the Concours, you would have us believe that you misunderstood the rules; you actually convinced some people and you must have found that very amusing. There is one point on which I believe you are telling the truth, and that is when you say that you did not set out intentionally to "differentiate" yourself from the others. No, you wanted to create a sensation. While your companions were wrestling in the thankless arena of the classroom fugue, you went off on maneuvers in an entirely different area which had more dazzling resources to offer. It was not a commendable action; fortunately its complete futility robbed it of the desired effect. An uninformed public, capable only of subjective appraisal, might have deemed your effort a great success; in the estimation of professionals, you merely did yourself a great disservice. You should have been disqualified from the competition; since that step was not taken, try to learn a salutary lesson from the generous gesture of your jury: with your capabilities, both natural and acquired, you have all that is needed for success, provided you will keep clearly in mind that shooting past the target is not the same thing as hitting it, and that a studied effort to make an impression is very often less effective than naturalness and simplicity.

Good luck,

Yours very truly
C. Saint-Saëns

Like many others, notable among them the music critic of the newspaper *Fémina*, Nadia was convinced that she would have been awarded the Premier Grand Prix had she been a man, and that she merited it; she decided therefore to try once again the following year, but once again met with failure, due in part perhaps to the continued antagonism of Saint-Saëns. Nor did it militate in her favor that her mother was conspicuously present at Compiègne during the residence period.

In any case, what could Nadia have gained by going off to the Villa Médicis? The incident of the preceding year, whether she had intended it or not, together with the secon prize awarded in spite of her infraction of the rules, netted her considerable publicity: all the newspapers gave her coverage, often including her photo; and, in January 1909, when she was only twenty-one, the Lamoureux orchestra gave two of her compositions their Paris première. The number of her pupils continued to increase, as did (though more modestly) the number of her concerts. And it was at

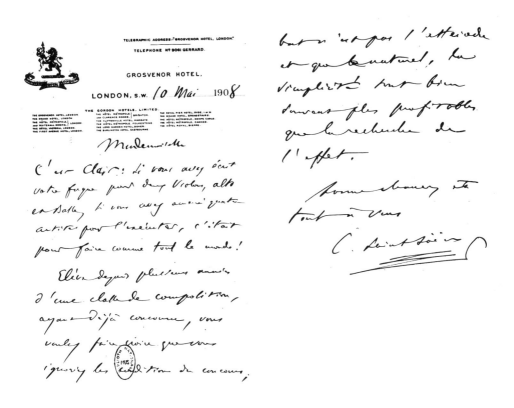

First and last pages of Camille Saint-Saëns' letter

this time that she began to compose with Pugno *Les Heures claires*, a cycle of melodies based on poems by Emile Verhaeren.

Musical collaboration of this sort was nothing new for Pugno: some ten years before, he had written the ballet, *Le Chevalier aux Fleurs* with André Messager. Actually, Raoul Pugno's career was a strange one. It has now been quite forgotten that this complete musician, born in 1852, initially gained fame as an organist and composer (oratorios, opéras-comiques, ballets), before launching tardily upon a career as pianist (he was over forty)—a career as astonishingly brilliant as it was late in beginning.

Since Pugno was reputed to be a man of many conquests, it was inevitable that his growing affection for Nadia Boulanger, young enough to be his daughter, should have caused idle tongues to wag: Nadia, and especially her mother, could hardly have failed to be aware of this fact. But they chose not to pay the least attention. Whatever

Compiègne, May 1908: Nadia wins second place in the Prix de Rome. Standing behind her,
Philippe Gaubert

24

may have been the degree of intimacy that developed between them, it is clear that Pugno and Nadia shared a very deep affection. In spite of the obvious advantages that Nadia might gain from having a musical godfather as famous and distinguished as Pugno, neither she nor he, without that sincere attachment, would have continued to work more and more frequently together and to live in close proximity in Paris, in Gargenville, in Saint-Jean-Cap-Ferrat, as well as on concert tours.

Pugno's support was helpful to Nadia when she sought and obtained the post of teacher of piano at the Fémina-Musica conservatory, an elegant establishment for young people of the best families. Nadia Boulanger already had her eye on the Conservatoire, but her ambition soared beyond being merely the assistant of Henri Dallier who had recently requested her to work with him there. In 1910, when a teacher was needed for the class in accompaniment, she did not hesitate to apply, regardless of the fact that she was only twenty-two (it is true that she was already well known as an accompanist and that the list of her partners kept growing by leaps and bounds from year to year: Paul Franz, Marthe Chenal, Jane Bathori, Germaine Martinelli, Germaine Cernay, Ninon Vallin, Suzanne Balguerie, Marcelle Bunlet, Claire Croiza, etc.). She persistently solicited the support of everyone who had, or whom she thought might have, any say in the matter. In doing so, it appears that she may not always have exercised suitable diplomacy, if one is to judge from the response she received from Claude Debussy, couched in such a way that beneath its surface flattery one can discern that touch of ferocity of which he was known to be quite capable:

> *Mademoiselle,*
>
> *Permit me to assure you that I do not see how I could be "systematically" opposed to your candidacy: quite on the contrary, I have a genuine appreciation of your talent, and am persuaded that no one is better fitted than yourself to fill the post for which you are applying.*
>
> *But surely you know what "committees" are like? The one involved in choosing you is no exception—any more than any other—to the rule which tends to make a committee appoint the very candidate who should have been carefully eliminated in the first place!*
>
> *So please excuse me in advance for my lack of influence, and accept my very best regards,*
>
> *Claude Debussy*

Nadia Boulanger did not get the appointment: her age, her sex, her sudden notoriety, perhaps even the flaunted endorsement of Pugno and the over-confidence it sometimes generated constituted too many handicaps. Oddly enough this peerless pedagogue, already far in advance of her time, and destined very quickly to reach the heights of influence and renown in this area, had to wait another thirty-five years

21. X.
   / 10.

Letter from Claude Debussy

before the doors of the Conservatoire would finally swing open to her as a duly appointed faculty member.

But if the year 1910 ended on a note of disappointment and wounded her self-esteem, which apparently healed quickly, it was also a year rich in positive events.

First of all was her decision to collaborate with Pugno on the music for Gabriele d'Annunzio's drama, *La Ville morte*, which had had its première in 1898 at the Théâtre de la Renaissance, starring Sarah Bernhardt. It is difficult to imagine today the amount of fame this Italian poet's work had brought him, despite a particularly stormy life whose scandalous episodes provided gossip for all Europe. Nadia Boulanger had met him at Pugno's and seems not to have been intimidated by his sulphurous reputation. She even formed a friendship with La Duse, one of the most famous of his mistresses,

26

Manuscript page from *La Ville morte* in Nadia Boulanger's hand

the one in fact who had talked him into writing for the stage. This openness on Nadia's part was in striking contrast to the severe, even puritanical stance that would later become an essential characteristic of her personality. For the moment, she had nothing but enthusiasm for this three-way collaboration which gave her the opportunity to spend a great deal of time with Pugno. From a letter written by d'Annunzio we learn that Pugno and Nadia divided up the task of composition, Nadia bringing "her fresh inspiration" to the female roles, and "Raoul taking care of the male element." The score was completed by the end of 1912, after a summer spent partly in Pugno's villa at Cap-Ferrat.

At the end of the summer of 1910, when the music of the first act was well under way, d'Annunzio confided to Nadia that it was his intention to ask Roger Ducasse to provide "the music for the songs, choruses, and dances for the *Martyre de Saint-Sébastien...*" but when the production had its premiere the following year the music was by Debussy, who had composed it in only three months (one of the conditions of a commission from the Ballets Russes that must have scared off Ducasse).

But it was also in 1910 at the Opèra that the same Ballets Russes first performed Stravinsky's *Firebird*. The discovery of this music, so unlike any other, was a major shock for Nadia, and her meeting, a few days later, with the young Russian composer (he was twenty-seven, barely five years older than she was) marked the beginning of a sort of adoration that lasted almost all her life.

A few weeks prior to this earth-shaking encounter, another event had occurred that, on the surface, appeared to be of no special importance: she had accepted a new pupil, a little girl of thirteen, Annette Dieudonné who would turn out to be her teacher's faithful companion until Nadia drew her last breath. Once Annette had finished her studies, circumstances combined with her natural disposition to make of her a vital, irreplaceable element in the Boulanger "organization." For almost seventy years Annette Dieudonné provided Nadia Boulanger with Friendship, Devotion, Fidelity, Efficiency, Protection (all with capital letters) to the point of folly—or saintliness. Nadia's life and career would assuredly not have been the same without the permanent presence of this "shadow of her shadow" who constantly stood guard over the memory of her mentor and friend until her own death in November 1991.

But 1910 marked yet another very special event: it was the year in which Nadia's little sister Lili, fragile in health and gifted to the point of genius, suddenly made up her mind to devote herself to composing. Nadia then took her seriously in hand, and was stunned to discover that within a few months Lili mastered, or grasped by instinct alone, what it had taken her several years to assimilate.

Nadia working on *La Ville morte* at Pugno's house in Cap-Ferrat (1912)

At Compiègne in 1913 with Lili, who had just won the Prix de Rome in composition

Prepared by Nadia, Lili entered the Conservatoire in January 1912. In spite of the interruptions occasioned by her bouts of illness, her studies were brilliantly executed. In July, 1913, at the age of nineteen, her crowning achievement was the coveted Premier Grand Prix de Rome—the first woman ever to earn this distinction!

Nadia as well as Lili revelled in this triumph, for Lili was, after all, Nadia's pupil. The Boulanger sisters were looked upon as prodigies, who upset accepted norms and customs. While on the one hand Lili was signing a contract with Ricordi to publish her musical works, guaranteeing for herself a significant measure of financial independence, Nadia was off to La Roche-sur-Yon to make her debut as conductor of an orchestra with none other than the illustrious Raoul Pugno as piano soloist!

For not only did Pugno and Nadia compose together, they played in concert together as well, most often at two pianos. Pugno's concert schedule was still a heavy one in spite of the state of his health, which left something to be desired. In 1912, the year he celebrated his sixtieth birthday, besides giving many recitals and orchestra concerts, he gave some forty sonata programs with Eugène Ysaÿe, the great Belgian violinist, and about ten concerts with Nadia. The two were in constant communication, and Pugno was at this time the axis around which Nadia's life revolved. She was always watchful that her illustrious friend be accorded due respect, and tended to bristle indignantly at any real or fancied slight, as the following letter (among others) bears witness. Written in May, 1913, and addressed to Maurice Ravel, it takes him severely to task:

> My dear Ravel,
>
> I saw Fauré this morning, and everything is in order. But before discussing our project, I have to tell you frankly how disappointed I was in the way you behaved yesterday. You know how much I like you and that's why I can't keep this bottled up. Pugno is an elderly man, and our friend, and I just can't stand seeing him treated without the same courtesy extended as a matter of course to everybody who comes to the house. Let me tell you how sorry I was that you left without even saying goodbye to him.
>
> Whatever your opinions may be, I'm sure you understand me, and now I want you to forget all about this note which I just had to write for my own peace of mind. . . .

Nadia was only twenty-five; Ravel, thirty-seven, and already Maurice Ravel! All the same, he responded by return mail, sounding like a little boy caught in the act of misbehaving:

Nadia Boulanger

Raoul Pugno

4, avenue Carnot—XVIIe

My dear friend,

I am doubly shocked:

1st) because, in spite of the fact that, as everyone knows, I am absent-minded, I have never until now committed an inadvertent act as enormous, as boorish, and as inexcusable.

2nd) because I just can't bring myself to believe that you and Pugno could ever imagine that I would behave so rudely on purpose.

As for opinions: let me tell you first that mine, like that of the majority of our colleagues, is that Pugno is a composer and a virtuoso of very great worth. But that's quite beside the point. Even if I had been introduced, at your place or anywhere else, to a fellow-musician of no talent at all, and younger than myself, I would consider it my duty, at the very least, to be polite.

Please give me Pugno's address and let me know when I can go to see him without causing him any inconvenience. I absolutely insist on going in person to apologize to him.

Please convey my apologies to your mother and sister as well, and know that I remain your respectful and devoted friend,

Maurice Ravel

Nothing more came of the incident, and Ravel never showed anything but respect and esteem for Nadia, who on her part always kept on good terms with him. Given her tendency to hold a grudge, it is doubtful that she removed all trace of the matter from her memory. With her consumate ability to equivocate, she would say to Bruno Monsaingeon towards the end of her life: "I knew Ravel . . . very well, and not at all. We were on very good terms, but unfortunately we never managed to establish that special bond which makes for good communication. To tell the truth, there was a side to Ravel that nobody ever knew. . ."

In 1913, Pugno took Nadia with him to Berlin to play, under her direction, the *Rhapsodie variée pour piano et orchestre* which she had written for him and which he had given its first public performance on February 9 of that same year at the Concerts Lamoureux in the Salle Gaveau, under the direction of Camille Chevillard. For the Berlin audience it must have been an extraordinary experience to witness a twenty-five-year-old French woman directing a German orchestra in a work of her own composition with, as soloist, one of the greatest pianists of the day!

More and more Pugno was linking Nadia's career to his own. A concert tour was arranged for the two of them in Russia where the public had always given Pugno a triumphal welcome; and despite a kidney operation which he had had to undergo at the beginning of the year, they set out to fulfil the engagement. Unfortunately the trip proved too strenuous for him in his weakened condition. They were obliged to stop in Berlin, where Pugno had to get medical attention for a severe attack of bronchitis. They did not arrive in Moscow until the evening before the first concert, which was scheduled for the twenty-third of December (with the soprano Mme Wieniawska participating). They were both physically exhausted, and also in "dire financial straits," to quote the S.O.S. telegram sent that very evening by Pugno to his friend Gustave Lyon. "Absolutely counting on your faithful friendship," the urgent appeal concluded. In order to arrive in time to meet his commitments, Pugno had greatly overtaxed himself. The following morning he appealed to Serge Rachmaninov to come to his aid:

> My dear great artist and eminent colleague:
>
> I am going to ask you for an immense favor.
>
> I arrived in Moscow yesterday to play tonight at the Notlem—the joint concert of Mme Wieniawski and Raoul Pugno.
>
> I just got here from Berlin where I spent the last five days in bed with an attack of bronchitis. The doctor thought I was well enough to travel, and let me leave. I immediately telegraphed my good friends the Wieniawskis that I was on my way.
>
> As a result of this 44 hour trip on top of so recent an illness, I was completely chilled by the time I arrived at the station and the fever started up again. Last night at midnight I called in the doctor, and this morning I consulted another very eminent one.
>
> They are both agreed that it is impossible for me to play tonight, absolutely out of the question.
>
> I immediately thought of you. Your name, so well known and so loved by the public, would be our salvation.
>
> Mlle Boulanger—who is a remarkable composer and performer—will be very happy to play the Mozart concerto with you, or anything else. And you would also have two solo numbers of your own choice.
>
> That, my dear colleague, is what I'm asking you to do. I know it is a very bold request—but artists are not only colleagues, they are brothers to some degree as well—and they do not mind helping each other out. My friend Wieniawski who will deliver this note to you will fill you in on all the details.
>
> I want you to know, and wish I could tell you myself, how deeply grateful I am to you.
>
> Raoul Pugno

Rachmaninov refused to play that night, and Nadia never forgave him. She struck his name from her memory, and her pupils quickly learned that this composer was never to be mentioned in her presence.

Hôtel Métropole. Moscou.
Гостиница МЕТРОПОЛЬ
МОСКВА.

18 Xbre 1913

Mon cher grand artiste
et confrère éminent,
Je viens vous demander un
immense service.

Je suis arrivé hier à Moscou
pour jouer ce soir à la
Noblesse — le Concert de Mme
Wieniawski et Raoul Pugno —

Je quittais Berlin où je venais
d'être cinq jours au lit avec
une bronchite — très souffrant.
Cependant, le médecin me
jugeant assez bien, m'a laissé

Letter from Raoul Pugno (3 pages)

36

partir — et j'ai immédiatement
télégraphié à mes bons amis
Wieniawski, que j'avisais.

Or — le voyage de 44 heures, sur
une maladie. tout récente
a fait que, dès mon arrivée à la
gare —, j'ai été glacé entièrement
et la fièvre m'a repris de
nouveau — Hier — à minuit, j'avais
un médecin — ce matin — j'en
ai vu un second — Tous ensemble.

Ils s'accordent tous deux à
dire que jouer ce soir pour
moi est impossible —
absolument impossible.

Or, immédiatement, j'ai
pensé à vous — Votre nom

célèbre et aimé du public
nous sauverait complètement.

Mlle Boulanger — qui est
une artiste compositeur très
remarquable — sera très heureuse
de jouer avec vous le Concerto
de Mozart — ou autre chose.
Et puis — vous aussi deux
numéros de Soli — à Votre choix

Voilà, mon cher Confrère
ce que je vous demande, c'est
très hardi — mais les artistes
sont non seulement des
Confrères — mais aussi un
peu des frères — et ils s'aident
Volontiers — Mon ami Wieniawski
qui vous remettra ce mot, vous
dira de vive voix tous les détails.
Je veux seulement vous dire
moi même, toute ma
reconnaissance devouée
Raoul Pugno

38

Nadia Boulanger and Raoul Pugno

And so the concert scheduled for the twenty-third of December had to be canceled. There would never be another. On the third of January, a pulmonary embolism felled Raoul Pugno.

Even discounting the great anguish Nadia felt at the sudden death of Pugno, one can well imagine the situation which confronted this young woman, isolated in a country whose language she could barely speak (Madame Boulanger had never wished to speak Russian in France), and without money or supportive friends—even though the Wieniawskis undoubtedly did what they could to be of help.

Nadia met the challenge with great courage, and was finally able to make the necessary arrangements to bring Pugno's body back to France, thanks to financial aid from a wealthy young woman who was a close friend of Lili's, Miki Piré.

After the interminable return journey, being in Paris once again was in every respect very difficult for Nadia. In spite of the presence of Lili and Madame Boulanger, who surrounded her with the most tender affection, Nadia felt very much alone. The countless letters which she received give some inkling of the profound upheaval in her life caused by Pugno's death.

Marthe Bouwens, the wife of Nadia's guardian, wrote: "May God give you strength to recover so that you can continue to take care of your little sister for whom you are the most important person in the world . . . . Thank you for having given us the privilege of knowing and loving your dear departed friend, whose memory is forever engraved in our hearts."

The letter that came from Claire Croiza, for whom Nadia often served as accompanist, and who would remain her life-long friend, was especially understanding: "My house is yours; you will have total privacy there to weep . . ."

And after a visit to d'Annunzio the day after her return from Moscow, she received this note:

> Dear friend,
>
> Your story and your grief-stricken face have left me deeply moved. I have always sensed beneath that mask of courage that you wear everyday, your true heroism—in the inner sense of the word. But, during those few moments of sincere closeness that we shared today, I saw you illumined by a grief so deep that—I cannot tell why—I found myself trembling with the same reverent awe that I experienced listening to certain notes of our Hébé, when you sang standing beside our great panting friend seated at the piano.
>
> I wanted to go out this evening to come to see you and listen to you again, but I am ill, and the doctor has told me to stay at home in this bad weather. I am alone,

Chère amie,

je suis encore tout
ému de votre récit et
de votre visage si doulou‑
reux. J'avais toujours
senti, à travers votre courage
de quotidien, votre véri‑
table héroïsme — dans le
sens intérieur du mot.
Mais aujourd'hui, pendant
ces quelques minutes de
sincérité fraternelle, je

vous ai vue toute éclairée
par une douleur si forte
que — je ne sais pas pour‑
quoi — j'ai tremblé de
la même émotion sainte
dont me remplissaient
certains cris de votre
Hébé, quand vous
chantiez debout, à
côté du grand ami

haletant.
Je voulais sortir ce
soir, pour venir vous voir
et vous entendre encore. Mais,
je suis souffrant; et le
docteur me prie de garder
la chambre, par ce mau‑
vais temps.
Je suis seul, en appa‑
rence; mais je porte le
poids de la vie, amis

entre vous deux.
Merci d'être venue.
Merci d'avoir eu confiance
en mon amitié.
Je vous reverrai demain.
Je suis avec vous, de
tout mon cœur, chère Na‑
dia. Votre
Gabriele d'Annunzio

44, av. Kléber.
Téléph. Passy 54.

Letter from d'Annunzio

to all appearances, but I am feeling the weight of life, seated between the two of you. Thank you for coming. Thank you for having relied on my friendship. I shall see you again tomorrow. I am with you, with all my heart, dear Nadia.

Your Gabriele d'Annunzio

Nadia herself would write a few months later, and repeat often that from then on "the memory of my great friend who has left us is the focal point of my life."

But this would not be so for long. Very soon there would be no more mention of Raoul Pugno. Certainly Nadia Boulanger could not erase their artistic collaboration of almost ten years, but she stopped talking about it; and the rest, so essential to her, was buried forever in her heart.

It is significant that Nadia Boulanger, who was obsessed with commemorating anniversary dates, never included those of Pugno, a curious "lapse of memory," which resembled another such lapse, no less surprising: she never commemorated the death of the late Ernest Boulanger, her own father, . . .

The war soon intervened, drastically disrupting both routine habits and newly-laid plans. Mobilization and the closing of most of the theaters brought to a halt the rehearsals of *La Ville morte*, which had just begun at the Opéra-Comique. This work, written "for four hands" as the poet liked to describe it, was destined never to be performed, although Nadia and d'Annunzio subsequently made some half-hearted efforts on its behalf. It was mentioned in the official advance notice for the 1916–1917 season of the Opéra-Comique, where one could read: "The Directors contemplate a very special revival with Mary Garden; the creation of several new, shorter works originating in the trenches; revivals of the *Dragons de Villars, Orphée*, the *Barbier de Séville*, etc., and—assuredly with the active collaboration of the great poet-soldier Gabriele d'Annunzio—a dazzling production of the *Ville morte*, the lyric work by Raoul Pugno and Mlle Nadia Boulanger. The sequence in which they are to be presented is yet to be determined. Performances will be given five times a week."

The declaration of war also precipitated Lili's return from Rome, along with Madame Boulanger, who had insisted on accompanying her daughter there. Her disconcerting presence at a stone's throw from the Villa Médicis had adversely altered its atmosphere, if not violated its rules.

After an extended visit in Nice with her close friend Miki Piré, Lili finally went back to Rome early in 1916, accompanied, as always, by her mother. In spite of the less than happy experience of her first sojourn there, Lili was determined to finish out her allotted time at the Villa Médicis, where she hoped also to enjoy the benefits of a more healthful climate . . . "if not, then the eucalyptuses of the Villa are no better than common ordinary shrubs," as Debussy wrote to Nadia.

Lili playing the organ at the rue Ballu

Lili surrounded by her comrades at the Villa Médicis

Lili's health did not improve, however, but grew progressively worse. Moreover, she was aware—although she did not talk about it to those close to her—that she did not have very much longer to live. The strength of character, the smiling resignation of this lovely twenty-three year old girl would have seemed heroic had it not been completely natural.

She now grew closer to Nadia, who from this time onward was busy pursuing a career made up of concerts, teaching, and writing. Taking advantage of every respite from illness, Lili never stopped composing. Nor did she back away from life. It was she who initiated the relief activity in which both sisters became deeply involved, giving comfort to soldiers, artists in general, and musicians in particular, from early 1915 on.

Lili and Nadia sought the aid of foreign artists and diplomats, especially those whose countries were not directly involved in the war, and were free to express their sympathy for France. Very naturally, the young women looked to North America.

What had started out as a private undertaking, a sort of family enterprise of limited scope, into which the Boulanger sisters had recruited their friends and those closest to them (like the Bouwens), quickly became an organization which, although still operated according to the original simple plan, had an official status, and the support of many celebrities. And thus it was that, towards the end of 1915, the "Comité Franco-Américain du Conservatoire de Paris" came into being, sponsored by Saint-Saëns—now reconciled with Nadia—Gabriel Fauré, Théodore Dubois, Emile Palhadile, Gustave Charpentier, Charles-Marie Widor, and Paul Vidal. A "Comité d'Action" was comprised of the latter two musicians, along with an American diplomat, Blair Fairchild (who was also a musician), and the two Boulanger sisters, with another American diplomat, Whitney Warren, as president. The headquarters and secretary's office were located at the Conservatoire, 14 rue de Madrid.

There is no doubt that this enterprise sowed the first seed of that extraordinary American career upon which Nadia Boulanger would embark some ten years later.

Under the pressure of events, Nadia was inevitably the one who took on more and more responsibilities of this Association. Although Lili, fleeing the excessive heat of Rome, returned to Paris at the beginning of summer in 1916, she never stayed there for very long at a time. Early in 1917, her mother carried her off to Arcachon, hoping that its vaunted climate would be good for Lili's precarious health. And it did seem to have some salutary effect which made it possible for them to return to Paris in the spring and spend the summer at Gargenville. But there she suffered relapse after relapse. After submitting to a hazardous operation by the famous surgeon Thierry de Martel she came back, drained of strength, to Gargenville, where she stayed until the onset of winter. In spite of her mother's presence and Nadia's constant

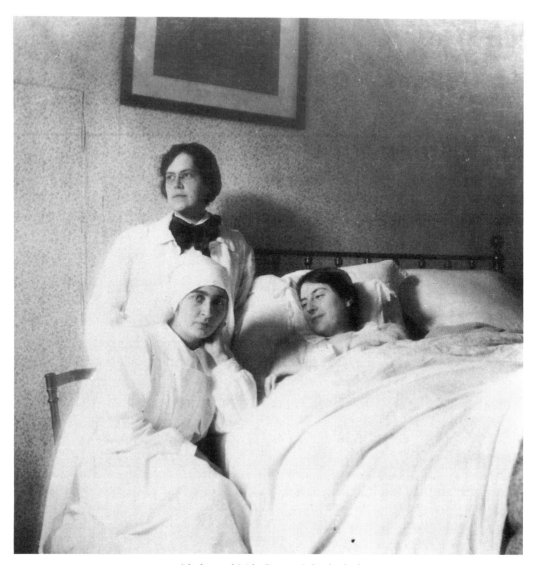

Nadia and Miki Piré at Lili's bedside

coming and going, Lili felt too isolated there, and insisted on returning to Paris . . . But, once again, she would have to leave: this time, in January, 1918, for Mézy, a little community near Melun, where she could be safe from the bombarding of the capital, and where she could be better cared for than at Gargenville.

There she remained. At Mézy, too weak to write, she dictated from her bed to Nadia a *Pie Jesu* of overwhelming simplicity for soprano, string quartet, harp, and organ. It was her last composition. She slipped away on the fifteenth of March, 1918. She was not quite twenty-five.

The ever-faithful Roger Ducasse had hastened to her bedside. After the separation of another war, he would remind Nadia of "those hours when I came to be with you, when I saw her for the last time, with the long-stemmed lilies on either side of her, our lily asleep in eternal peace, and you and I, dear Nadia, brought her back to Paris, where only regrets, flowers, and tears were waiting for her! Those tears, yours and mine, forged a bond between us which time has no power to weaken . . ."

Lili Boulanger left a significant body of work, composed in less than six years during which she fought a constant battle with illness and pain. Between the initial cantata, *Pour les funérailles d'un soldat*, composed in 1912, which preceded the *Faust et Hélène* that won her the Prix de Rome the following year, and the final *Pie Jesu*, her major works consist of *Renouveau*, a vocal quartet; three *Psaumes*; the *Vieille Prière bouddhique*; two symphonic poems; songs, including the *Clairières dans le ciel* cycle, based on poems by Francis Jammes; and, lastly, an unfinished opera, *La Princesse Malène*, on a text by Maurice Maeterlinck.

"In the history of music," Jacques Chailley comments, "her case is quite possibly unique. When one speaks of composers who have died prematurely, one is hard put to find among them any of distinction who had not passed their thirtieth birthday with the possible exception of Pergolesi, who was twenty-six at his death. Schubert lived to be thirty-one; Mozart, thirty-six; Purcell, thirty-seven. Not one of them, at the age of twenty-four, had written a work of the scope of the three *Psaumes*."

The death of her younger sister left an indelible mark on Nadia. From then on she dedicated part of her life to the promotion of Lili's works. At thirty, she found in this endeavor a holy mission: "She was so superior morally and spiritually, so pure . . . She became an example for me."

Everything connected with Lili became sacred. Each year, March 15 had its special liturgy, both a private mourning and a public ritual. Those hostile to Nadia Boulanger—and they were never in short supply during the course of her long life—in their eagerness to disparage whatever she did or failed to do, chose to interpret her devotion to the memory of her sister negatively, alleging that it probably stemmed from Nadia's remorse for having failed to do enough for Lili while she was alive, particularly during the last years of her brief life.

This reproach appears groundless. Those who express surprise that Nadia was not constantly with her sister need to be reminded, quite to the contrary, that she multiplied her visits both to Rome and to Arcachon, and that she tirelessly made the trip from Paris to Gargenville, and later to Mézy, in order to spend as much time as possible with Lili.

Actually, one cannot help but admire the way in which Nadia, torn between her various activities, managed to organize her schedule so that the deep bond of affection which linked her to her "little sister" was never jeopardized. Nor is it to be forgotten that, although Lili enjoyed some private income, it was by no means adequate to defray the expenses of her illness, and the task of meeting the family's material needs was shouldered by Nadia, and by her alone.

The allegation that she neglected Lili was just one of the many malicious accusations that Nadia's exceptional and long-lasting success engendered, arousing as it inevitably did a good deal of envy and jealousy.

It is true that Nadia's habitual manner, rebuffingly austere, often triggered a response of surprise, uneasiness, even shock. Hugues Cuenod, whose acquaintance with her spanned almost half a century, said that "she had a lot of heart, and even more brains. And perhaps she had even more principles than she had brains." And, in an effort to define the limits in human relationships imposed by this personage who, besides, took pleasure in maintaining an aura of mystery, Cuenod added: "She always remained inaccessibly aloof." Doda Conrad, another long-time friend who tended to characterize people in terms of their humility or modesty, classified Nadia as "humble . . . but not modest."

"Les Maisonnettes" at Hanneucourt-Gargenville

It is also true that Nadia, no doubt with shrewd ulterior motives, constantly cultivated wealthy and worldly connections. If, in her heart of hearts, she must often have been critical of these acquaintances, others were no less critical of her for seeking them out, and dubbed her mercilessly "little sister of the rich."

It is equally true that Nadia earned a great deal of money (should that be considered a crime?), for which she was also reproached because it put her in a position to withstand being influenced. To quote Cuenod once again, "In her likes and dislikes, she was absolutely unshakeable." And that was true in every aspect of her existence. Quite understandably, those who never managed to become part of her "clan" also never managed to forgive her for excluding them. And then, although she was always on her guard, she did occasionally make mistakes, trusting now and then in some man or woman who did not hesitate to betray her confidence.

But Nadia also inspired life-long friendship, devotion, and fidelity which often bordered on the fanatic. Two such friends who played a significant role in Nadia's life were Walter Damrosch and the Princess Edmond de Polignac.

During the first half of this century, Damrosch, although little known in France, was a musician of front-rank importance in the United States. When the United States entered the war against Germany in April, 1917, Damrosch was the head of the New York Symphony Orchestra. It was then that he created the "American Friends of Musicians in France," an association whose representatives were immediately welcomed into the bosom of the "Comité franco-américain du Conservatoire." And in 1918, Damrosch came to France to direct a prestigious 14th of July benefit concert for the Red Cross, given in the concert hall of the Conservatoire under the patronage of General Pershing. The "great symphonic orchestra" assembled for the occasion included the best talents of the Colonne Concerts, the Lamoureux, and the Pasdeloup: outstanding on the program were the *Variations symphoniques* of César Franck, with Alfred Cortot, and the third *Symphonie* of Saint-Saëns, with Nadia Boulanger as organist.

The fifty-five year old Damrosch, then at the peak of his brilliant career, was apparently thunderstruck by the rich personality and many gifts of the young Nadia: the authority, the culture, the range of this young musician seemed all the more remarkable to him because she was a woman and barely thirty years old.

Damrosch was insistent that Nadia come to the United States. "I have still not given up hope that you will come to America this year," he wrote her on December 4, 1918, a few days before giving the first American performance of Lili's *Faust et Hélène* at Carnegie Hall.

49

With Walter Damrosch, visiting the ruins of Reims in 1919

For her part, Nadia was quite visibly taken with Damrosch. Years later, on the occasion of the fortieth anniversary of the founding of the *Ecoles d'art américaines de Fontainebleau*, July 8, 1961, she still recalled, "When he passed by, everything came alive. His enthusiasm was contagious. He always gave so much of himself that he got back from others what he expected of them."

It is true that, even though Nadia Boulanger's first visit to the United States had to be put off year after year, the idea of these *Ecoles d'art américaines* in France had been generating in Damrosch's mind from the time of his first visit, while the country was still at war.

As soon as peace had finally been restored, Damrosch returned to Paris, where a very distinguished group of musicians—André Messager, Alfred Cortot, Nadia Boulanger, Pierre Monteux, Henri Casadesus, Auguste Mangeot—organized a brilliant reception in his honor to thank him for the "important services he had rendered to French art in America," and for the "assistance he had afforded our musicians sorely tried by the war."

Thanks to his position and his reputation, Damrosch was able to continue that assistance on an even greater scale than before. He raised substantial funds from his compatriots to contribute to the restoration of areas devastated by the war. In the summer of 1919, with Nadia as his guide, he visited the most severely damaged sites, especially Rheims, where the cathedral had been ravaged by fire, and the music school, like most of the city, utterly destroyed.

Damrosch was also responsible for creating at Chaumont a school for orchestra conductors, the administration of which was entrusted to Francis Casadesus. This school was the forerunner of the *Ecole de Fontainebleau*, which would be founded two years later, under the aegis of an American Committee organized through the efforts of Damrosch, and presided over by Mrs. J. M. Tuttle (who made a generous personal contribution). It was directed, like the Chaumont school, by Francis Casadesus.

On both sides of the Atlantic the project was vigorously promoted. The School of Music, housed in the Louis XV wing of the château, was inaugurated on June 26, 1921, in the presence of Camille Saint-Saëns and a number of his distinguished fellow

The early days at Fontainebleau School: Mlle Boulanger's class

51

musicians, including Charles-Marie Widor (who gave an organ recital at the Jeu de Paume on this occasion). Walter Damrosch was there, of course, as were the principal American donors, including Harry Harkness Flagler and Mrs. Tuttle.

Ninety students registered, chosen from among the most brilliant in each state of the Union. Their talented young teachers (like Robert Casadesus or Jean Morel) were supervised by their illustrious elders, such as Paul Vidal, Lucien Capet, Isidore Philipp, André Hekking, or Widor. Nadia Boulanger, now thirty-three, was entrusted with the class in harmony, reputedly a dry and arduous discipline, which she proceeded to revolutionize.

Teaching from the piano keyboard, Nadia constantly illustrated the theoretical points she was making with examples drawn from her phenomenal musical background and aided by her no-less-phenomenal memory. Many students officially enrolled in other classes gravitated towards Nadia's, irresistibly drawn by her authority, her enthusiasm, and her scope. It was no longer a matter of dry as dust harmony: it was music. Nadia herself would put it in just those words, towards the end of her career: "I teach music. That's the simplest way to put it—I teach music."

The drawing room at 36 rue Ballu

In her apartment on rue Ballu, Nadia gave her classes in harmony at first on Fridays, then on Wednesdays from the fall of 1921. The success of those classes made her change them to classes of "musical analysis." And musical analysis was exactly what it was: she had a genius for it. Jean Françaix compared her to an impassioned and fascinating watchmaker. It is true that she had been more or less trying out her new teaching concept for two years. In the autumn of 1919, Alfred Cortot (who had given up his piano class at the Conservatoire the preceding year) together with Auguste Mangeot, had founded the *Ecole Normale de musique*. They put Nadia in charge of the classes in organ, harmony, counterpoint, and—later on—the history of music.

This caused a sensation, for no woman up until then had ever held such positions. And for Nadia it was a sweet triumph that made up for being rebuffed at the Conservatoire. Very quickly her classes became so popular that it was necessary to limit enrollment.

From this time on, Nadia's concept of pedagogy took on clear definition. In the *Monde Musical* of January 1920, Nadia wrote: "My goal is to awaken my students' curiosity, and then to show them how to satisfy that curiosity. I want to make it clear that their dedication to music must come first, before their dedication to their own careers. My personal opinion is not what matters: it has no importance whatsoever."

She always put the emphasis on bringing out the individual personality of her students, not on influencing them: "Each student requires a different approach; one must try to understand each one." At the same time, Nadia was inflexible in matters of technique. She never permitted the least inattentiveness. She did not hide her admiration for Leopold Mozart whom she considered to have been "so unfairly criticized" for having managed to "bring out the best in his son" by teaching him "to love what was difficult." But she was totally tolerant of what was individual style and expression.

For her students, each lesson was an adventure. They never knew in advance how it would go. Her lessons reflected the astonishing eclecticism of this unpredictable woman for whom music was life itself. It is easy to understand the powerful attraction of her courses, so unconventional in form at this time.

In 1921, Aaron Copland was among the first pupils at Fontainebleau. He was twenty years old, and had enrolled in Paul Vidal's composition class. Out of curiosity, he sat in on one of Nadia's classes; completely won over by the way she dissected the score of *Boris Godounov*, Copland never missed another of her classes the whole summer long. He even made up his mind—though not without some hesitation—to ask her for private lessons: "No composer had ever had a woman teacher. It wasn't Nadia Boulanger I was worried about—it was my reputation!"

53

Hôtel
de France & Choiseul
239-241, Rue St Honoré
(Place Vendôme)

Adresse télégraphique:
Francheul-Paris

Tél. Central 41-92

May 30/1923

Dear Medora

I'm in the midst of all kinds of preparations, packing &c &c. but must snatch a moment to write to you and to thank you for your very dear note.

Your friendship means so much to me and makes your promised visit to

Paris is one of my greatest joys.

If you could send me a word of introduction to the Directress of the Villa Medici I should be very grateful.

Widor did not give me an introduction. He did not think it necessary, but I should like to feel that I am entering the portals of the Villa Medici under your

protection, wing. Transport and the children join me in sending you and your dear mother our love.

We expect to leave tomorrow morning and arrive at the Hotel Eden, Rome by June 5th or 6th unless all of our pneus explode somewhere en route!

As always yours affectionately

Walter Damrosch

Letter from Walter Damrosch

54

Completely convinced, Copland stayed on in France with Nadia Boulanger for three years, even spending some time as house-guest in her rue Ballu apartment. He put his sojourn to further advantage by working at the piano with Ricardo Viñes. In addition, Nadia introduced him to the international world of music which Paris was then the hub. In particular, she intopduced him to Serge Koussevitzky with whom she was working closely at the very moment when, as a result of this Russian-born conductor's successes at the Paris Opera, he was named head of the Boston Symphony Orchestra, a post Pierre Monteux had just vacated. This was the sort of connection most precious to a very young composer!

Copland's attachment to Nadia Boulanger never wavered. From the beginning, spontaneously, he became for her—almost before such a thing actually existed—a most effective "public relations" man in the United States.

There is no doubt that the immediate success of the *Ecole de Fontainebleau* was in great measure due to Nadia Boulanger's personal magnetism, which was to prove a powerful drawing card to several generations of young American musicians. In ever greater and greater numbers they came to France to work with her. Fontainebleau was usually their first point of contact, often followed by extended sojourns in Paris.

For nearly fifty years, the rue Ballu apartment became a sort of Mecca. The studious pilgrimages to it were interrupted only during the years of World War II; once peace was declared, they resumed immediately.

Walter Damrosch had not been mistaken in lavishing upon his young colleague an affectionate admiration which he made no attempt to hide. He even asked her to put in a good word for him before he visited the Villa Médicis!

May 30, 1923

My Dear Nadia:

I'm in the midst of all kinds of preparations, packings, etc., etc., but must snatch a moment to write to you and to thank you for your very dear note.

Your friendship means so much to me and seeing you on my annual visits to Paris is one of my greatest joys.

If you could send me a card of introduction to the Director of the Villa Médicis I should be very grateful.

Widor did not give me an introduction. He did not think it necessary, but I should like to find that I am entering the portals of the Villa Médicis under your protecting wing. Margaret and the children join me in sending you and your dear mother our love.

*We expect to leave tomorrow morning and arrive at the Hotel Eden, Rome by
June 5th or 6th unless all of our pneus explode somewhere en route!*

As always affectionately,

> *Yours,*
>
> *Walter Damrosch*

For Nadia Boulanger these post-war years were full of intense activity which
kept on accelerating, causing her to live at a frantic pace. Not a single moment was
wasted. It would be impossible to count how many hours she worked each day. Her
nights were short. She lived her life at the same reckless speed she drove her cars,
which was not very reassuring, for she admitted that when she was behind the wheel
she never thought of anything but music! "I'm always hearing notes, I'm always
thinking notes." Everywhere, under all circumstances.

It was one of her American pupils who taught her to drive, and in order to be
in two places at once—to be in Gargenville where her mother spent the summer,
and at the same time also be in Fontainebleau where she didn't take up residence in
the château until later on—she made the trip between Gargenville and Fontainebleau several times a week at the wheel of her own car, which reinforced her image
as a strong, independent woman.

Beginning in 1919, she added one more string to her bow, writing critical articles
for the magazine *Le Monde musical* which Auguste Mangeot had recently founded.
She had little taste for this task, and had nothing but scorn for most of her fellow
critics: "Why should I take an interest in what X, who has never produced anything,
thinks about what Y has created—whether it be bad or good?" According to one of
her former students, a well-known and opinionated critic was holding forth on
modern music one evening at a dinner party; he stopped long enough to inquire of
Nadia Boulanger, who wasn't saying a word, whether or not she agreed with him.
She answered: "I don't understand a word of what you are saying—it might as well
be Greek or Chinese. But please go right ahead. I don't mind—it's like listening to
poetry!"

Her collaboration with *Le Monde musical* was destined to end in short order, for
even though she was then at her peak, the tempo she forced upon herself took its
physical toll. She was never actually ill, but from this time on she began to suffer from
those violent migraines with which she lived for the rest of her life. For the most part
she managed to disregard her ills, never cutting down on her commitments, which
grew even more demanding in 1920 when she took on the class in music history at
the Ecole Normale that Paul Dukas had given up.

She was very happy to take his place because she felt a sincere admiration for the composer of *L'Apprenti sorcier*, *Ariane et Barbe-Bleue*, and *La Péri*—an admiration which she never lost an opportunity to express, in spite of the fact that, ten years earlier, when she had first applied to the Conservatoire, he had not given her the support she asked for (although he had avoided the issue graciously). Times had changed, and it was with total spontaneity that she congratulated him on his advancement in the order of the Legion of Honor. He answered her immediately:

Royan, August 13, 1923

Dear Mademoiselle,

I cannot tell you how much your little note touched me, and how much pleasure it has brought me—pleasure due infinitely more to the kind thoughts expressed than to the occasion that prompted them, honestly! And you can't keep me from congratulating myself on the circumstances which brought me so fine a reward as your sensitively enthusiastic letter. In these troubled times, you will never know how much it means to a musician—who is, alas, growing old (as this rosette bears witness)—to be applauded by a musicienne so ardent, accomplished, and artistic as yourself.

A thousand thanks, dear Mademoiselle, with all my very best regards.

Paul Dukas

It seemed as though everything Nadia Boulanger turned her head to at this time was successful, and the following period was also manifestly favorable for her. There was something different about her now, outwardly attested by a radical change in her costuming: the severe suits of former days were suddenly replaced by brightly patterned dresses—totally unlike the strictly somber attire she would adopt only a few years later. This unexpected sartorial fantasy surely points to a specially significant digression in her life: photos taken of her at this time show us a young woman of rounded contours, with sparkling eyes, full of laughter and smiles—unmistakenly a happy woman.

Was there some special reason for this sudden blossoming? Or did Nadia for a moment simply let down her guard and relax that stern self-control she had always exercised in the past and would shortly once again impose upon herself?

Did some special friendship or perhaps an even stronger emotion, some carefully kept secret, bring her that serene fulfillment which, for each of us, changes the prism through which we look at life and the world?

Or was it simply that Nadia caught the free spirit—as if it were contagious—of those young Americans at Fontainebleau, all the more uninhibited because they were liberated from the puritanical strictures of their homeland?

Royan 13 Août 1923

Chère Mademoiselle

Je ne puis assez vous dire combien votre petit mot me touche et me cause de plaisir, infiniment plus par les sentiments qu'il m'exprime que par l'événement qui en motive l'expression, assurément! Et vous ne m'empêcherez pas de me féliciter moi-même de l'occasion qui m'a valu la lettre si délicatement enthousiaste que vous m'avez écrite. Aux temps troublés que nous vivons, vous ne savez cuire de quel prix est pour un musicien, hélas vieillissant (la preuve: cette rosette!) l'adhésion d'une musicienne aussi ardente, aussi accomplie et aussi artiste que vous l'êtes! Merci mille fois, chère Mademoiselle avec tous mes hommages et ma meilleure sympathie

Paul Dukas

Letter from Paul Dukas

The sun dress

ADMINISTRATION :
13 - RUE - DE - TOCQUEVILLE - PARIS - XVIIe
TÉLÉPHONE : WAGRAM 18-03

PARIS, le 29 sept. 83.

ma chère amie,

J'allais précisément vous écrire et vous témoigner mon désir, personnel de jouer cette année, au châtelet, une des œuvres voulu- de votre chère Lili. rous apprès le 9 octobre (je marie Simone le 8) me faire parvenir la partition d'orchestre du Psaume 129, je l'étudierai avant de soumettre votre proposition à mon comité et je vous ferai part de notre décision

- Il est bien entendu d'ailleurs pas, que l'œuvre ne comporte pas de chœurs! nous ne pourrions en assurer les frais... et pour vous encourager d'ailleurs à monter les œuvres de jeunes symphonistes, l'État vient de nous réduire de 5000/ notre maigre subvention! et en est de même chez Lamoureux

Letter from Gabriel Pierné, continued opposite

60

Vous viendrez n'est-ce pas, entendre l'œuvre de Pierné à la répétition?

Mes meilleurs souvenirs pour vous et votre chère maman.

Gabriel Pierné

It would be futile to attempt to answer such questions at this juncture: only a few years later the dark cloak would descend upon Nadia once again, this time for good, when her mother died. It was as though the death of Madame Boulanger— surely an event to be expected in the natural course of things, painful though it undoubtedly was—served as a final call to order, making Nadia from then on the prisoner of a rigid code of rules nevermore to be transgressed.

There still remained for Nadia, in the middle of that long life so preoccupied with mourning, a decade or so of brighter years that might be compared to a brief scherzo in a great symphony of gray and black.

The death of her mother did not prevent Nadia from devoting herself as much as ever before to the memory of Lili, and to the immortalizing of Lili's works, which she not only played in her own concerts but also convinced others to play as well—as we can see in the following letter from Gabriel Pierné, who reveals in passing that problems with Parisian bureaucracy were nothing new; in a letter written later on, he would burst out once again: "Oh! How music is badly handled and treated with indifference in our beloved country!":

September 29, 1923

My dear friend,

I was just about to write you to let you know that it is my personal wish to play one of the works of your beloved Lili at the Châtelet this year. Would you please see that I get a copy of the orchestra score of Psuame 129 after October 9 (I'm marrying Simone on October 8). I'll study it before submitting your suggestion to my Committee, and will let you know our decision. It is my understanding that the work does not involve a chorus—it doesn't, does it? We could not guarantee the funds for

61

that—besides, the State has just reduced our subsidy by 50,000 francs! A fine way to encourage us to serve as a showcase for young symphonic talent! It's the same thing at Lamoureux!

You will come to the rehearsal to hear the works of Pierre Menu, won't you?
Fondest regards to you and to your dear maman.

Gabriel Pierné

In 1920, Nadia was still composing: she created a few songs with texts that Miki Piré had dedicated to Lili, and she also set to music some poems by Camille Mauclair whose friendship she was then cultivating. These represented to all intents and purposes the final appearance of Nadia the composer, giving the lie to the legend—which she herself may have to some degree encouraged—that she had ceased to compose when Lili died.

The truth is that at a certain moment in her life Nadia Boulanger was obliged to make a choice among her many activities. She would never give up her concerts, although more and more her role tended to be as director rather than performer. On the one hand, she was passionately committed to her teaching, and her pedagogical gifts were literally bursting into full bloom; on the other hand, her gift for composition seemed to her less obvious, especially when she compared her work to Lili's.

"My music wasn't good enough to be beautiful, nor bad enough to be amusing," she used to say good-naturedly to those who regretted her decisions to give up composing.

Fauré was one of those, but without ill-will. After winning her prizes at the Conservatoire, Nadia had indeed grown apart from him, which wounded him deeply. But when she sought to renew their friendship, when he was turning over the reins of the Conservatoire to Henri Rabaud, Fauré welcomed the overture magnanimously. On September 15, he wrote to her:

. . . these past fifteen years your excessive discretion made me think that you had grown indifferent to me, or that, perhaps, you had changed the direction of your work. You'll have to make up for that: your charming letter, which gave me such pleasure, is a good start.

Nadia had doubtless resented the fact that Fauré had not supported her applications to teach at the Conservatoire as strongly as she would have liked while he was in charge. But when Fauré died November 4, 1924, laden with honors but terribly isolated because, as a consequence of having grown deaf, he had shunned society for years, it was Nadia Boulanger who was asked to deliver his eulogy at the national funeral services held at the Madeleine.

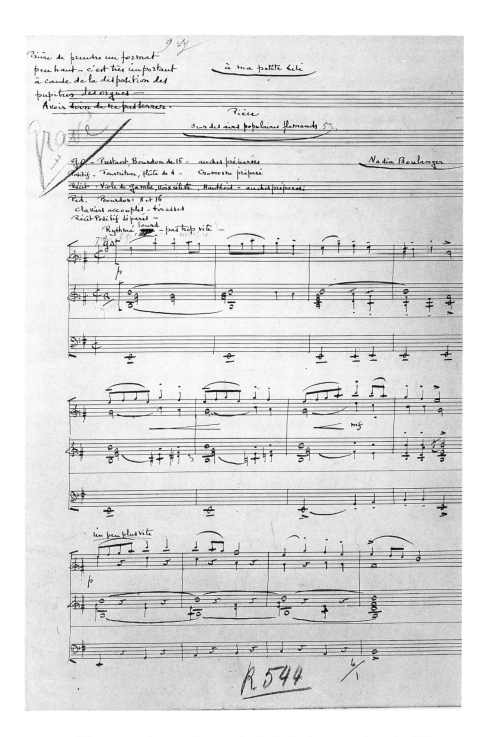

Manuscript of a piece for organ by Nadia Boulanger, dedicated to Lili

A few weeks later, Nadia embarked at Cherbourg on the steamship *Aquitania*: Damrosch's efforts had finally come to fruition. On December 31, 1924, he was waiting at the pier, surrounded by newspaper reporters, to welcome her to New York.

Very careful preparations had been made for this first trip, not only by Damrosch—at whose home Nadia stayed while in New York—but also by young Copland who had written a symphony with organ for her which she would introduce in New York under the direction of Damrosch. A month before she sailed for the United States, Copland had written her:

November 24

Dear Mademoiselle Boulanger,

They tell me you are sailing as early as the 17th. Mais, c'est merveilleux!

Yesterday I saw Mr. Damrosch and played him the work. He seemed quite enthusiastic, especially about the second movement. He said he thought it was well orchestrated, but that the title ought to be "Symphony" and not Little Symphony. When I suggested that the proportions of the work were not those of a big symphony he said that it was by the ideas and not by the size that he would name it, and since the ideas were in no sense 'intime,' to call it Little Symphony would only mislead people to expect something entirely different. So from here and now we shall call it a Symphony—là! The parts are now being copied and I hope everything will be in order by the time you arrive.

Already I have seen one concert announced that you must not miss—at the Metropolitan Opera House, Paul Whiteman is to give a concert of jazz music—nous y serons. I won't go on to tell you all the other events you must not miss, you will know of them soon enough.

Give my regards to Madame Boulanger. Tell her that if she knew of all the devoted friends you have in America, she would not worry about you one bit.

Bon voyage et à bientôt

A.C.

P.S. If, by any chance, we should miss you at the boat, telephone to me— Trafalgar 0185

Billed by both press and publicity as "the famous French organist," Nadia opened her series of concerts with a recital in Philadelphia on January 9 at the mammoth organ in the Wanamaker Auditorium, where all great organists were expected to try their hand. But it was in New York two days later that Nadia made her real debut with the New York Symphony Orchestra under the direction of Walter Damrosch, playing an organ concerto by Handel, and Copland's *Symphonie*, as well as Lili's *Pour les funérailles d'un soldat*. The critics gave this concert rave reviews.

135 W. 74 St.

Nov. 24 [1925?]

Dear Mademoiselle Boulanger —

They tell me that you are sailing is early as the 17th. Mais, c'est merveilleux! Yesterday I saw Mr. Damrosch and played him the work. He seemed quite enthusiastic, especially about the second movement. He said he thought it was well orchestrated, but that the tittle ought to be 'Symphony' and not Little Symphony. When I suggested that the proportions of the work were not those of a big symphony, he said that "it was by the ideas" and not by the size that he would name it; and since the ideas are in no sense 'intime', to call it Little Symphony would only mislead people in expecting something entirely different. So from here and now we shall call it a Symphony — Là! The parts are now being copied and I hope every thing will be in order by the time you arrive.

Already I have seen one concert announced that you must not miss — at the Metropolitan Opera House, Paul Whiteman is to give a concert of jazz music — nous y serons. I won't go on to tell you all the other events you must not miss, you will know of them soon enough.

Give my regards to Madame Boulanger. Tell her that if she knew of all the devoted friends you have in America she would not worry about you one bit. Bon voyage et à bientôt.

A.C.

P.S. If, by any chance, we should miss you at the boat, telephone to me — Trafalgar 0185.

Letter from Aaron Copland

Between January 9 and February 25, not only did she keep some twenty-six concert commitments—besides the New York concert and the Philadelphia recital, she traveled to Vassar College in Poughkeepsie, to Cleveland, Houston, Saint Louis, Minneapolis, Indianapolis, Cincinnati, Chicago, and Boston (where the program of the New York concert with Damrosch was repeated but this time with the Boston Symphony Orchestra under the direction of Koussevitzky)—but, at the same time, she gave a number of lecture-recitals, introduced by Walter Damrosch, which drew most favorable attention to her and were outstandingly successful.

This thirty-seven year old French woman captivated those who heard her, so brilliant and clear was her thought, even though it was delivered in words that were often approximate, a precipitous delivery, and a very pronounced French accent which she was never able to (or perhaps never really wanted to?) overcome.

In front of the organ console at the Wanamaker Auditorium in Philadelphia, between the Italian organist Marco Enrico Bossi (left) and Marcel Dupré (right)

One of her trump cards was the fact that she was so completely at home at the piano, for, although she was not an extraordinary virtuoso (her association with Pugno had given her an accurate measure of her own talent), she was nonetheless an excellent pianist.

The text of the three lectures that she gave at Rice Institute (*Modern French Music*, *Debussy*, and *Stravinsky*) was taken down in shorthand and transcribed the following year, giving tangible proof of the interest she had aroused.

This first contact with America was indisputably a great success for Nadia, although not a financial one. The modesty of the monetary reward was, however, in large measure compensated for by the contacts she was able to make, thanks especially to Damrosch. She established many connections, not just in academic and musical circles, but also among the wealthiest members of the aristocracy. They fought over her, competing for her attendance at high society gatherings in New York. This was the beginning of that ambivalence in Nadia's life style that her detractors did not fail to criticize: she demonstrated on the one hand the most rigorous professionalism, and, on the other, a penchant for fashionable drawing-rooms.

Without further delay, the Curtis Institute of Philadelphia offered to create a permanent chair of music for Nadia. It would seem that she found this offer both very attractive and very flattering. She hesitated before refusing it, but refuse it she did

The "Boulangerie" at Gargenville

(just as, in 1927, she would refuse to accept an important series of lectures that would have taken her all across the United States). Her main reason for declining in both instances was her mother's failing health. Madame Boulanger was suffering from the first onset of what was undoubtedly Parkinson's disease, making it quite out of the question for Nadia to think of bringing her to the United States, and still more unthinkable to contemplate leaving her behind. So Madame Boulanger continued to reign over the world of the rue Ballu in Paris and over the summers in Gargenville, where Nadia soon began to invite her favorite students and also those who were most devoted, for in Gargenville everyone had to pitch in and help, even with domestic chores.

Twelve years would pass before Nadia Boulanger came back to America. But in the interim America came to her via Fontainebleau. The reputation of Fontainebleau kept growing by leaps and bounds (and in 1924 it widened the scope of its activities to include architecture and the plastic arts). Among the best known of the students who flocked to Nadia Boulanger's classes at that time were Walter Piston, Virgil Thomson, Theodore Chanler, Robert Delaney, and Roy Harris, most of whom immediately became her fervent supporters. Some of them, when they in turn became teachers, sent her their own pupils, thus bearing eloquent witness to the unique superiority of her teaching. Copland was especially diligent in this regard. It was he who recommended Marc Blitzstein to her (their relationship proved to be pretty difficult). Walter Piston also sent her many students, among them in 1933 one of his most talented—Elliott Carter.

All Nadia Boulanger's pupils were always proud to mention their years of study with her: it was a sort of irrefutable badge of distinction which served as the best possible letter of introduction everywhere.

Much later on Leonard Bernstein, who had been not quite seven years old when Nadia first visited the United States, discovered her with admiration. When, in Boston, he went on to become the assistant of Koussevitzky after having first been his pupil, he wrote to her (in French): "You are a truly great lady, and the debt we all owe you can never be repaid. Now I see for myself at last what all my composer friends have been talking about for so long."

The majority of them did, indeed, credit Nadia Boulanger with having inspired contemporary American music.

Without a doubt, between 1924 and 1937, the date of Nadia's second trip to America, her "Boulangerie" (one of her students came up with the name) became, in matters of musical instruction, the most exclusive "club" of international renown.

68

Not just anyone could get into the club: only those with talent . . . or money! "Mademoiselle" (as everyone now called her) ruthlessly turned away applicants who had neither. Only very occasionally, and then just for a limited period of time, she might make a rare exception. She protested good-humoredly that she had yet to encounter a student who had both talent and money! So she accepted some wealthy candidates who paid handsomely for the privilege, making it possible for her to offer very generous conditions (or to waive the fee altogether) in the case of someone particularly gifted in whom she took a special interest.

Among those born musicians, who were often brought to her very young, was little Jean Françaix who was only ten when he came to her in 1922: he would grow up, in every sense of the term, beneath Nadia Boulanger's affectionate rod.

Although she herself always remained secret, inscrutable, even with her protégés, the strong hold she had over her students went beyond the bounds of the usual teacher-pupil relationship. She sought to penetrate the world of those whom she taught, even venturing at times to intrude upon their private lives, or to orient them in the direction of the Catholic faith, which for her was a source of moral strength and firm convictions.

But in matters of religion as in matters of music, she had no use for those who were mediocre—"What is impossible is mediocrity!" Nor did she have any use for flatterers. To a student too anxious to please her, she retorted impatiently, "I don't know what YOU want. Until I know what you want, you simply do not exist for me as far as music is concerned."

It is characteristic that after the student revolt of 1968 in France, she said: "If I had been protesting, I would have fought not for the *right* to have my own opinion, but for the *obligation* to do so. One must learn ways to express one's own personality—if it exists!"

She could be even more emphatic on this point: "You have to be yourself. Influences that are badly assimilated are dangerous. Debussy's personality was so strong that by influencing those who came within his orbit he prevented a lot of them from being themselves. They thought they were continuing *Pelléas*: but all they were doing was making parallel chords. And there are also some who keep on making the repeated chords of the *Sacre du printemps*. They're just running along behind the band-wagon. . . ."

She applied the same logic to herself. Over and over again, she defined her conception of the role of the teacher as, basically, "a draconian technique. Without an in-depth knowledge of technique, a musician is incapable of expressing any part

Nadia and her mother at Gargenville around 1930

of what he or she feels most intensely. And that is where the teacher comes in. All that a teacher can do is develop in students faculties that will enable them to handle their tools effectively (insisting that they give undivided attention, that they be always present, that they learn to persevere): but the teacher has no active role whatsoever in what students do with that tool."

Thus she disclaimed any intention of exerting personal influence over her students. And she never failed to keep that distance she deemed essential. For example, when the Argentinian, Astor Piazzola, arrived in France in 1954 to work with Nadia Boulanger, she was not at all impressed with his laborious compositions. But one day his friends mentioned to "Mademoiselle" that he improvised tangos and played them better than anyone else. Then "Mademoiselle" insisted (she had to insist, because at first Piazzola refused) that he demonstrate for her what he could do in this form. After she had listened to him for a long time, she told him in all earnestness: "That's your field! Give up symphonic music and dedicate your energies to the tango." He went on to become king of the tango. Of Nadia Boulanger he would say that he thought of her as his second mother.

She always strove to maintain this clear perception of what she could or could not do for her students, respecting the personal aspirations of each, provided they were sincere. But she had no use for the weak ones; once she found them out—and this was true for those who performed under her direction as for her own students— she went after them relentlessly, pushing them to the limit in a way that seemed cruel: many were those who burst into tears beneath the lash of severity, sometimes even in the presence of other musicians. Even some well-known artists fell victim to these humiliating scenes, so painful for a third party to witness, but which left Nadia Boulanger as unmoved as a block of marble.

In 1927 she celebrated her fortieth birthday. By this time she had acquired a prestige so great that everyone who composed or who wanted to compose came to her.

In 1928 when Ravel was spending some time in New York, George Gershwin took advantage of the opportunity to meet him. Ravel wrote Nadia about him on March 8:

> *Dear friend,*
>
> *Here's a musician endowed with the most brilliant, the most captivating, perhaps the most profound qualities: George Gershwin.*
>
> *His universal success is not enough for him any more. He aims higher. He knows that for that he needs something he doesn't have. But were we to teach him what he wants to learn, it might destroy him.*

71

THE BILTMORE
NEW YORK

8/3/28

[Handwritten letter in French by Maurice Ravel]

Letter from Maurice Ravel

Will you have the courage, which I dare not have, to take on this terrible responsibility?

I'm supposed to get back around the first of May, and will come to discuss this with you.

In the meantime, I send you my most cordial regards,

Maurice Ravel

A magnificent letter, teaching a beautiful lesson in modesty: it is true that Gershwin's *Rhapsody in Blue* and *Piano Concerto* had come out three years earlier.

But what humility on Gershwin's part as well! This young musician, only thirty years old, was obstinately determined to undertake at last those in-depth musical studies of which he had been deprived. In June 1928 he wrote to Nadia Boulanger:

Monday

Dear Mademoiselle,

I am in Paris for a short visit and would like very much to meet you again. I believe we met when I was here two years ago, through the Kochanskis. I have a letter to you from Maurice Ravel.

Please be so good as to telephone me at the Hotel Majestic or write me a note letting me know when and where we could meet. With all good wishes I am,

Most sincerely,

George Gershwin

Gershwin was not one of those "running along behind the bandwagon"! She received him at the rue Ballu apartment, but had the same reaction as Ravel, and declined the awesome privilege of taking him on as a student: "What could I give you that you haven't already got?" And she convinced him that he must continue writing *his* music.

That same year, 1928, at the Ecole Normale, she gave a series of lectures entirely devoted to Beethoven, with musical illustrations by the famous Calvet quartet. The venture was an enormous success, giving proof once again of her charisma as a lecturer, a fact well established two years earlier when she gave a series of lectures on Debussy's *Pelléas*, Fauré's *Pénélope*, and Dukas' *Ariane et Barbe-Bleue*.

Letter from George Gershwin

These subjects represented only one facet of her musical interests. For at this period she was still very receptive to all the currents of contemporary music: as early as 1923 she had become an active member of the International Society of Contemporary Music, founded the year before; and most of the concerts she organized included works by contemporary composers, some who were her own pupils, and some who were not.

For example, the name of Olivier Messiaen appears among them. In 1931 she presented the premiere of his *La mort du nombre* for soprano, tenor, violin, and piano (with the composer himself at the piano: "No one ever at the piano but me," he had stipulated).

But their relationship deteriorated in 1934 shortly after the annual mass commemorating the death of Lili. It took place at the Trinity Church, where Messiaen (who had been the official organist since 1931) after beginning with a Bach chorale, proceeded to improvise "all through the ceremony"—conduct for which he was vigorously reproved. He wrote a letter in which he attempted to justify what he had done, pleading "not guilty," and adding with all the brashness of a twenty-five year old, "I'm awfully sorry you were disappointed. I readily understand that any program—even if it were ultra-magnificent—would seem to you unworthy of your sister's memory." Ever afterwards there was an undercurrent of hostility between them, although they maintained a surface politeness that testified to their genuine mutual esteem.

Nadia also took an interest, initially, in the work of Schoenberg and followed the careers of Berg and Webern; she even made them the subject of some of her courses. In all probability she attended at least one of the concerts of Jean Wiéner in 1921 or 1922, in the course of which Schoenberg's *Pierrot lunaire* was performed several times, with Marya Freund as soloist, under the direction of Darius Milhaud. Since the Wiéner concerts featured Stravinsky's works prominently, it is all the more likely that Nadia would not have missed them.

Was it actually because of Stravinsky and because of his intense dislike of Schoenberg—which was fully reciprocated—that Nadia Boulanger promptly turned her back on the "serialists?" She had never cared for "systems" in music, but it is quite conceivable that her desire not to ruffle the "great man" influenced her negative response to "serialism." Later this would prove somewhat embarrassing to her when, after World War II, and under the growing influence of Robert Craft, Stravinsky himself would launch into dodecaphonism.

In any case, Nadia was always very cautious in her appraisal of serial music. She alleged that one did not as yet have sufficient perspective on it to make a definitive judgment. Toward the end of her life she would qualify her opinion even more; extrapolating from *Lulu*, she admitted: "there is, alas, some music that I don't like. Even though such music may have the traits of a masterpiece, even though it may be completely successful and worthy of respect, I just cannot love it because it in no way corresponds to what I am capable of feeling."

But from the very first note she could and did love the *Firebird*, and then *Petrouchka*, and *The Rite of Spring*. During the war of 1914 Stravinsky had written *Renard* and *L'Histoire du Soldat*; then came, in 1920, the *Symphonie pour instruments à vent*, dedicated to Debussy; *Mavra* in 1922; *Noces* and *L'Octuor pour instruments à vent* in 1923; and *Concerto pour piano et orchestre d'harmonie* in 1924. . . .

Most of these works had been subsidized in one way or another by Princess Edmond de Polignac. Beginning in 1910, she had met, welcomed, and defended Stravinsky, and most especially had provided him with financial support. She had him create works for her which often were heard for the first time at grand soirées in the extraordinary drawing-room of her impressive residence on rue Cortambert.

We are too prone nowadays to forget the important role which this astonishing woman played in France, her adopted country, where she put her immense fortune to good use. For she was not only a great patron of the arts—painters and musicians alike: less well remembered is her generous support of such prestigious organizations as the

In 1928, beside her new Hotchkiss

75

Institut Pasteur or the *Collège de France*, not to mention her philanthropic role, from 1911 onward, in the construction of low-income housing—what today one would call social welfare projects.

The twentieth acknowledged child of Isaac Singer (gifted inventor of the sewing machine, whose incredible life might well provide the plot for a most fantastic adventure novel), Winaretta was born January 8, 1865 in New York, the second child of Isaac's fifth official wife. If he was typically American, this particular wife, who was his last, was a French woman of Irish descent. It was almost by chance that Winaretta was born in the United States, which she left for Paris at the age of two with her parents. She was not to return until sixty years later, in 1927, and then only for a short visit with her friends, the Trefusis. She discovered, thus, the land of her birth ... and decided that she would never again set foot in it!

In 1887, at the age of twenty-two, she had married M. de Scey-Montbeliard, motivated in large part by the desire to escape from the supervision of her mother, with whom she did not get along. But it seems no one had thought to tell Winaretta what such a union involved in terms of conjugal duties—which, horrified, she

The Princess de Polignac at her organ in the music room of her home on the avenue Henri-Martin

categorically refused to assume—to the consternation of her husband. A divorce was granted in 1891, and she obtained an annulment from Rome the following year.

She married again, however, toward the end of 1893, this time to Prince Edmond de Polignac, thirty years her senior. She knew that she would not have to fend off this new husband, notorious for tastes kindred to her own. So they lived amicably side by side, united by a very real affection born of shared tastes for the arts in general and music in particular. (Edmond de Polignac had emerged from the Conservatoire with a Premier Prix in composition the very year in which his wife was born, and counted among his friends all the composers of the period; and the birthday present Winaretta asked for when she turned fourteen was a private performance of a Beethoven quartet.)

And so Winaretta Singer became Princess de Polignac (to whom Ravel dedicated his *Pavane pour une Infante défunte* in 1899). And she remained Princess de Polignac after the death of her husband in 1901—three years before the completion of the imposing residence she had decided to have constructed at the corner of avenue Henri-Martin and rue Cortambert (now George-Mandel and Pasteur-Marc-Boegner, respectively). For almost forty years this elegant neoclassical edifice was to be one of the citadels of Parisian art, wit, and wealth, not to mention politics, for Raymond Poincaré was a frequent guest there and Ambassador Maurice Paléologue was no less welcome as friend and valued counselor. In fact, they were the ones who helped the Princess establish the Foundation that bears her name.

Nadia Boulanger did not gain admittance to this temple right away. Or perhaps she held herself back, prompted to keep her distance because of the reputation of "Aunt Winnie," as those close to the Princess often called her. But Nadia's friendship with Stravinsky, a frequent guest there, inevitably led her one day to avenue Henri-Martin. Since 1917 the Princess had begged her to come and play the organ she had had installed in the grand music room. Here the Princess herself spent a great deal of time, seated at the keyboard of one of her pianos or of the organ, at times alone, at times surrounded by a host of first-rank musicians: Clara Haskil, Jacques Février, Francis Poulenc, Henri Sauguet, Maurice Ravel, Eric Satie, etc. But it was only from 1924 on that Nadia Boulanger began to be a regular visitor.

In 1927 she was there for the first private performance of Stravinsky's *Oedipus-Rex*, just before its public premiere at a concert in the Sarah-Bernhardt Theater. The text by Jean Cocteau—also a close friend to the Princess—was translated into Latin by the future Cardinal Jean Daniélou.

The whole thing had been financed by Aunt Winnie, the work having been at first intended for Diaghilev; but the animating genius of the Ballets Russes, then in declining health, was reluctant to undertake it. By a curious coincidence, his death

Nadia with "Aunt Winnie" at Jouy-en-Josas, around 1932

two years later occurred at the very time Nadia Boulanger was making her real entrance into the world of the Princess de Polignac.

She became more or less its chapel master, making herself indispensable from then on for everything pertaining to the musical activities of this Maecenas, whose week-end residence at Jouy-en-Josas she now frequented as well as the Princess's palace in Venice. She fell into the habit of bringing with her to rue Cortambert the most gifted of her pupils. This rare honor often won for the young musicians a commission from the Princess who, despite her own very sure taste and instinct in matters of art, deferred with total confidence to the musical judgment of Nadia Boulanger, who became for her the most invaluable of friends.

Over the course of the years, Nadia introduced into this circle such young unknowns as: Igor Markevitch (in 1929; he was seventeen years old); Marcelle de Manziarly (in 1930); Jean Françaix (in 1934); Dinu Lipatti (in 1936). Obviously, here was an incomparable springboard for those who knew how to take advantage of it. But this preferential treatment did not fail to stir up jealousy and uncharitable comment.

The savage portrait of young Igor Markevitch in Virgil Thomson's memoirs is a case in point: having characterized Markevitch derisively as "the new little genius," Thomson goes on to complain that "this Russian, barely out of his teens, had been discovered three years before, in 1928, by Diaghilev, then promoted by Cocteau, taken in hand by Nadia Boulanger, sanctified by Prunières, protected by the Princess de Polignac, and subsidized by the Viscountess de Noailles."

Despite its venom, this summation was not too far from the truth, giving a reasonably accurate picture of the world of wealth, of more or less intimate in-fighting and intrigue which, though highly conducive to the flourishing of the arts, was hard to reconcile with the image of severity which Nadia Boulanger normally projected. But she always managed to see only what she wanted to see, and, not indifferent to the rising tide of celebrity, she went with the flow.

The feminist movements made an effort to enlist her. She resisted their blandishments. But—even had she wanted to—there was no way she could stop the women-readers of *Minerva* from voting her "Princess of Music" in 1928, an event publicized in the newspaper by a lyrical feature article in six-columns abundantly illustrated.

At the same time the American magazine *Musical America* sent feature writers to Gargenville to prepare an in-depth article on "Mademoiselle" and her pupils. It is true that she did a great deal for those pupils of hers, constantly including their works

Photograph signed and dedicated by the 21-year-old Igor Markevitch

in the programs of the concerts she organized and often directed. In 1926, for instance, she gave a concert which stirred up a great deal of interest, consisting solely of the works of American musicians: Herbert Elwell, Aaron Copland, Walter Piston, Theodore Chanler, George Antheil, and Virgil Thomson bore living witness to Nadia's conviction that the future of music lay with the United States.

Almost all of them were her students. From year to year their numbers grew. They came from the four corners of the globe, some of them bearing illustrious names—like François Valéry and Soulima Stravinsky, offspring of Paul and Igor respectively, whose friendship Nadia zealously cultivated.

But the Wall Street crash of 1929 had its effect on the stream of young Americans heading for France. For several years the number of students coming to Fontainebleau diminished; even more important, the financial support without which the School could not continue to function was very precarious in those years between the crash and the outbreak of World War II, which some people were beginning to perceive as inevitable. When Ravel took over from Widor as Director of the School in 1934, he was faced with a grim situation.

This development did not appreciably affect Nadia Boulanger. If Fontaine-bleau's demands upon her decreased to some degree, this was compensated for by increased activity on behalf of the Princess de Polignac. She helped the Princess get through a period of depression as uncharacteristic of her as it would have been of Nadia herself. "Neither of us has any patience with stupid lamentation," Aunt Winnie would write to Nadia, once the crisis was passed, "If I managed to get back on a more or less even keel, it's almost entirely thanks to you, to your genius, to your magnificent example, and to your unwavering kindness, the thought of which moves me deeply and fills me with infinite gratitude."

The Princess and Nadia both responded with intense enthusiasm to the 1931 Paris premiere of Stravinsky's *Symphonie des Psaumes*, commissioned the year before by Serge Koussevitzky to celebrate the fiftieth anniversary of the Boston Symphony Orchestra. Nadia had followed the composition of the piece with passionate interest.

Works by Stravinsky figured constantly in the private concerts which the Princess had Nadia organize regularly, leaving the choice of programs entirely up to her. The first of these concerts took place in June 1933—just a year after Nadia Boulanger was awarded the Legion of Honor, thanks to her old friend Roger Ducasse who campaigned for her, actively assisted by Cortot.

These first programs were very classical, consecrated to Bach and Vivaldi. But they evolved rapidly: the salon concerts served as a sort of laboratory which afforded

At her organ in the rue Ballu

Nadia Boulanger the opportunity to perfect those astonishingly eclectic programs, which she would later give everywhere. "I didn't do it just to be provocative," she said, "It was an inevitable development."

Circumstances made it possible for Nadia to gather around her a little group of first-rate musicians, most of them vocalists, who remained with her faithfully for many years. At first there was the opera singer Maria Modrakowska, who performed her own songs and those of Lili in 1931, but she participated only at the beginning of the venture. Above all, there was Marguerite di Pietro, the daughter of Jeanne Lanvin.

Polignac she changed her name from the com-
nche, which suited her to perfection. She brought
uty, charm, and elegance, but also the sensitivity
f celestial purity.

drew Marie-Blanche into her orbit, as she did so
enor Hugues Cuenod—brought along by a friend
antata courses in 1931, and an assiduous partici-
e were the sisters Irène and Nathalie Kedroff, the
(Irène had been a student at the Ecole Normale,
In 1935 she encountered the bass Doda Conrad,
And other artists kept coming along to complete
pecial mention; and then there were, at intervals,
Paul Derenne.

, this remarkably musical and remarkably homo-
less number of concerts under Nadia's direction,
ensemble recruited to meet the specific needs of

(left) and Marie-Blanche de Polignac in 1933

each program, but always top-flight performers. Very often, however, the vocal ensemble sang without accompaniment, or with Nadia alone at the piano.

The Polignac concerts brought her others, notable among them were those at the homes of other patrons of the arts such as Henri and Isabelle Gouin, or Count Jean de Beaumont. But, from 1934 onward, Nadia was also put in charge of organizing afternoon concerts on the average of about once a month, for the very aristocratic Cercle Interallié; and two years later she would take on the kindred task of inaugurating and shaping the pattern for the morning concerts held at the Hotel Georges V.

The ever-increasing number of concerts obliged Nadia to vary her programs continually. She often achieved this variety by reviving older works and presenting them for rediscovery. The period was one in which forgotten music was actively sought. It was around 1925 that Wanda Landowska, in residence at Saint-Leu-la-Forêt, began her valiant and determined effort to bring back the harpsichord and its repertoire.

Claude Crussard and her instrumental ensemble Ars Rediviva, in turn recreated the music of the seventeenth and eighteenth centuries in their concerts: their 1935 recordings brought them sudden popularity, and awakened in a widening audience a taste for this music so long neglected—despite the efforts Vincent d'Indy had made in his time to resuscitate some of the chefs-d'oeuvre. (The Ars Rediviva has been unjustly forgotten since the air tragedy in Lisbon in 1947 which took the lives of most of their members, together with their director, Claude Crussard.)

Interest in the music of yesterday was in the air, and Nadia Boulanger did more than her share to promote it, bringing into the limelight a number of composers and works totally unfamiliar to the public. Not only did she introduce to her audiences most of the cantatas of Johann Sebastian Bach, and revive works such as *La Résurrection* by Schütz, or Carissimi's *Jephté*, but she was also almost solely responsible for the rediscovery of the Monteverdi madrigals: in 1937, at the request of His Master's Voice, she made five recordings consisting exclusively of a group of those madrigals, which she had tried out in concert performances.

She had to be persuaded to make the recordings because she had no more love for phonograph records than for writing: she was convinced that both tended to arrest concepts in mid-flight (or to fail to do justice to them entirely), whereas thought, like music, and like life itself, is always in process of evolving.

But Doda Conrad took matters in hand and managed to overcome Nadia's reluctance, ably assisted by the Polignac clan with Aunt Winnie in the lead and also Jean; equally supportive was Pierre de Monaco, a fervent admirer of Nadia's. He became one of her most faithful friends, giving her the run of the princely palace after

The jury of the International Society for Contemporary Music, meeting at Albert Roussel's home in 1936. From left to right: Arthur Honegger, Nadia Boulanger, Arthur Hoérée, Albert Roussel, Henry Prunières, Darius Milhaud

the war, where, for more than thirty years she was in full charge of the musical arrangements for all important ceremonial events.

No pains were spared in the production of the madrigal recordings: Paul Valéry wrote an introduction for them, and François Valéry supplied a brief analysis of Monteverdi's works. And in December of the year they came out (1937), Nadia Boulanger's madrigal records were awarded the *Grand Prix du Disque*.

It is hard to imagine today what an undreamed-of success these recordings enjoyed from the moment they first appeared. It was overwhelming (the name of Nadia Boulanger became a household word) . . . and it lasted—a half century after their initial production as 78 RPM records, they were made available in 33 RPM, and today in compact discs.

The only regret one might have is that the figured bass was played on the piano rather than on the harpsichord. No one seemed bothered by it at the time, and later on when anyone expressed surprise to Nadia at the absence of the harpsichord, she answered that the thought had simply not occurred to her. Authentic restoration had yet to become as fashionable as it later became; but it is possible that Nadia chose the piano rather than the harpsichord because the latter instrument, then used so rarely, was too exclusively linked to the name of Landowska. And no love was lost between the two women.

However that may be, Nadia Boulanger's international reputation was now fully assured. Two years earlier, she had sustained the profoundly shattering jolt of her mother's death on March 19, 1935. It came only four days after the seventeenth anniversary of Lili's passing. (Madame Boulanger, in spite of her extreme weakness, had insisted on being present at the mass at Trinity.)

Because of the proximity of these dates, the month of March from then on became a month of mourning for Nadia, marked not only by the immutable rite of the anniversary mass (consecrated henceforth to both the departed loved ones), but also by her total withdrawal from social events, or any activity, except for the most essential professional commitments.

This two-fold mourning, reflected in the somber clothing which Nadia wore from then on, never permitting herself the least sartorial whimsy (even though, from the time she first met Marie-Blanche de Polignac, all her concert dresses were designed by Lanvin), had consequences of varying importance.

Her outward appearance was much altered: a glance at the astonishing photograph of Nadia with Stravinsky on the ocean liner two years later suffices to show

Return from the United States in 1937 with Igor Stravinsky

how greatly she had changed: everything about her was deliberately austere, if not ascetic.

As far as practical everyday duties were concerned, Nadia began, and would continue until the day of her own death, to keep the account books of daily household expenses, as her mother had done, keeping track of even the most trivial of expenditures down to the last penny. This task was added to another which she had imposed upon herself since 1910—that of recording by hand, in four books (one per quarter), which grew bulkier each year to the point of becoming monstrous, the origin of every letter she received, and the destination of every letter she sent out, adding at holiday time, lists of presents given and received.

One cannot help but be astounded at such organization in a woman who sometimes taught from seven in the morning to ten in the evening, who gave (and therefore had to prepare) concerts at a rate unknown to many virtuosos, and who, in spite of all this, had a social life that was far from negligible.

Perhaps this hectic pace may not have been unrelated to her physical transformation as well: her rounded contours disappeared, causing a sharpening of her features, which was accentuated by the wearing of *pince-nez*, that gave her face a severity that she knew how to bring into play whenever she wanted to make a strong impression.

But that still was not all: after the death of her mother, Nadia Boulanger systematically commemorated all the important anniversaries of her friends and acquaintances. Marked on an outsized calendar at each date of the year were the births and deaths (of spouses, of children, of relatives); and each day, after consulting her calendar Nadia would write in her own hand (at least as long as she could see well enough to do so) either a few lines or an actual letter—depending on the status of the recipients, or on the degree of intimacy that linked her to them—sharing their joy, or more often grieving with them over the memory of the lost loved ones. This task involved on the average a good half dozen cards or letters every day, Sundays and holidays included, and no two missives were exactly alike, despite their acutely painful repetition.

Now it happened that towards the end of the sixties, this precious calendar disappeared! Despite Nadia Boulanger's extraordinary memory, it had to be painstakingly reconstituted: her devoted slaves spent many weary months at this thankless task, indispensable to the perpetuating of the rite. Unfortunately, they were not always certain of an exact date, and some mistakes were repeated year after year—as in the case of Darius Milhaud, who did not quite manage to conceal his irritation after receiving for the third time in succession congratulations well in advance of his actual birthday!

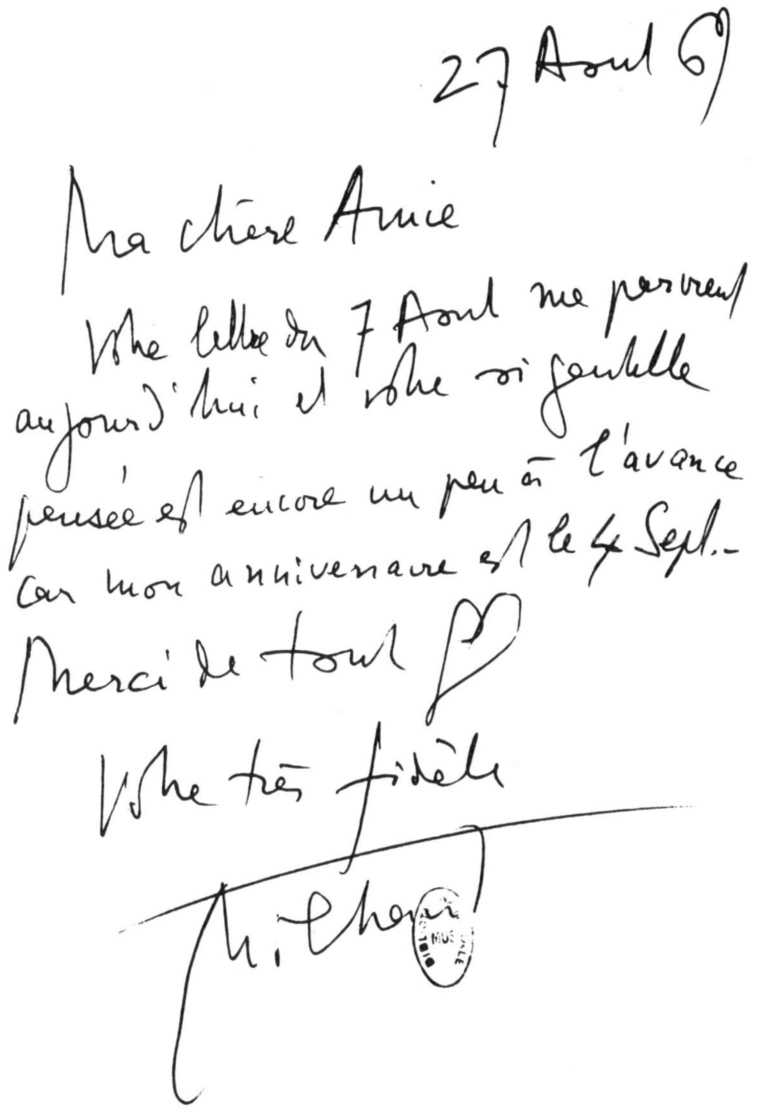

27 Août 69

Ma chère Amie

Votre lettre du 7 Août me parvient aujourd'hui et votre si gentille pensée est encore un peu en l'avance car mon anniversaire est le 4 Sept.—

Merci de tout ♡

Votre très fidèle

Milhaud

Letter from Darius Milhaud

August 27, 1969

My dear friend,

    Your letter of August 7 has just reached me today, and your very sweet thought is still a bit premature, since my birthday is the fourth of September.

    Thank you with all my heart.

                              Your very faithful Milhaud

There was something chilling about the routine nature of this well-organized perpetuation of memories. "The cult of misfortune was a way of life to her," said Hugues Cuenod, whose affection for Nadia did not keep him from seeing her clearly. But, all the same, there was, in this woman, who chose to cherish this cabal of sad events, an undeniable sincerity, and perhaps the black moleskin book represented for her a sort of extended family which gave her some relief from "the burden of loneliness?" That was how the Princess de Polignac expressed it; on the occasion of the death of her own older brother, whom she adored, the Princess had written to Nadia: " . . . as we grow older we grow weary, and it is perhaps more difficult to pull ourselves out of the depths of certain sorrows (but what I'm saying is absurd, for I know that it is not easy *at any age!*)"

The many letters from the Princess after the death of Madame Boulanger bear witness to her great heart and her deep affection for Nadia, which she expressed with much simplicity and sensitive restraint.

In these letters there were sometimes amusing anecdotes about little intimate dramas, like the one which took place in Venice at the palace of the Princess, between two male musicians, friends of Nadia, whose romance was broken up by "that clever demolition-expert, Jean Cocteau." And the Princess went on to emphasize "the underhanded means by which J.C., like Colette's old Léa, using flattery, and pandering to egotism, etc., brought about a probably permanent separation." (If she tried on this occasion to thwart Cocteau's designs, his jibe at her expense is more readily understood: he liked to call the Princess "Mother Dante," [La mère Dante] alluding to her profile, which did indeed call to mind that of the father of *The Inferno*.)

How did Nadia Boulanger respond to such stories? We do not know, for, even supposing the Princess may have kept these letters, her archives have been scattered and are for all intents and purposes lost for good—which is regrettable. The reserved appearance that Nadia Boulanger sought to maintain might seem to justify the conclusion that she would have no interest in minor escapades of this sort, nor in hearing about them, but in the last analysis one cannot be sure: it must be remembered that, until the death of her mother, Nadia was not at all averse to having fun, and the parties given at the rue Ballu apartment and in Gargenville were very lively, with no stinting of wine or merriment. The death of Madame Boulanger seems to have frozen something in Nadia, even though from time to time humor still broke through, as it did when, directing rehearsals of old songs whose lyrics were slightly off-color, she would caution her vocalists—with her lips half-smiling, half-pursed: "Don't articulate too clearly!"

If the death of Madame Boulanger brought Nadia's very real loneliness into clear focus, it gave her, at the same time, complete freedom of movement: at forty-eight years of age the future belonged to her.

Recording of a television program at the BBC in London, 10 November, 1937

    While Nadia was busy preparing the Monteverdi recordings, the Princess de Polignac arranged for her to visit London in November 1936, opening the doors of the Royal Philharmonic Orchestra for her, while Doda Conrad at the same time opened those of the BBC.

The five days of recording for the radio presented no special problems, and the broadcasts were a great success. Equally successful, was the concert given in Queen's Hall on November 24 with the Royal Philharmonic; but in this case there were obstacles that had first to be overcome.

Never since its foundation, which dated back more than a century, had this orchestra been conducted by a woman, and its director, duly forewarned by the Princess, had to expend a great deal of time and diplomacy smoothing the way for Nadia Boulanger: her welcome at the first rehearsal was chilly—a mixture of curiosity and hostility on the part of the instrumentalists, masked by a thin veneer of politeness. But she managed to impose her authority immediately, and her professionalism impressed the musicians, already taken by surprise at a program so out of the ordinary, consisting of virtually unknown works, including the *Résurrection* by Schütz, *Dithyramb and Hymn* by Lennox Berkeley (a work commissioned by the Princess de Polignac from this English pupil of Nadia's), and Fauré's *Requiem*, of which this would be—astonishing though it may seem—the first performance in England.

The house was far from being full—the imminent abdication of Edward VIII created a less than propitious climate—but at the end of the concert the instrumentalists were among the first to applaud this "top-flight conductor," as the music critic of the *Times* described her in his column the following day.

These successes no doubt had a role in her sudden decision to return to the United States, a decision reinforced by the fact that she obtained a grant form the *Minister of National Education* to go over and study American methods of teaching music.

It was largely thanks to Louise Talma, a devoted student from Fontainebleau, who was to become one of Nadia's most loyal friends, that arrangements for the trip were made on the spot. Accompanied by Gisèle Peyron and Hugues Cuenod, Nadia Boulanger put the month of April, 1937—which she spent on the other side of the Atlantic—to good use: she gave concerts, recorded radio broadcasts, gave lectures in the eastern United States (New York, Philadelphia, Washington, and Boston), to say nothing of teaching a few classes at Harvard University. The programs were astonishing, ranging from Monteverdi and Schütz to Poulenc and Françaix, including, en route, Bach, Mozart, Rameau, Ravel, and Debussy. But they were fascinating, and when she set sail for home she had proven herself to be what Damrosch (who had once again welcomed her with open arms) said she was: "the most distinguished woman musician of France."

This brief and successful visit gave her the opportunity to renew old ties and to develop new ones, which resulted in plans for another American tour of much greater scope to take place the very next year. Nadia also profited by her visit to help Igor

At the head of the Royal Philharmonic Orchestra of London

Stravinsky in every way possible. He was going through a period of very straitened circumstances, and was in fact at that very time touring America giving piano concerts to earn money. She got him a commission from her friends, Mr. and Mrs. Robert Woods Bliss: he composed for them the *Dumbarton Oaks Concerto*, named after their Georgetown estate. Stravinsky and Nadia met again aboard the *Paris* en route back to France, where they disembarked on May 12, 1937.

On January 25, 1938, Nadia once again sailed for America, this time on the *Champlain*. The few intervening months had been divided between Fontainebleau, Gargenville, and the rue Ballu; she gave several concerts as well, including another one at Queen's Hall in London, this time to a packed house. She also recorded radio programs, some in Paris and some in London, and gave an incalculable number of private lessons. Especially noteworthy was her new recording of the Brahms vocal quartets, the *Liebeslieder Walzer*, with the piano-four-hand accompaniment provided by Nadia and young Dinu Lipatti, whose career at twenty, under her strict discipline, was already remarkable. "Everything you predicted for him has come to pass," the Princess de Polignac, dazzled by Lipatti's performance, wrote to her the following year.

When she left from the Gare Saint-Lazare, and also when she docked in New York, surrounded by her complete vocal ensemble, Nadia Boulanger was treated like a star. Forty concerts were scheduled; from early February to the middle of May alone

January 25, 1938: departure of the boat train at the Gare Saint-Lazare. From left to right: Dinu Lipatti, Hélène Vergniaud, Lucie Rauh, Annette Dieudonné, Irène Kedroff, Marcelle de Manziarly, Nadia Vergniaud, Nadia Boulanger, Cécile Armagnac, Léo Préger

she gave some sixty lectures and classes, which meant an average of at least one appearance a day—with the exception of March 15, the sacred anniversary, which was kept free from all engagements, both professional and personal.

In the concert programs, works by Francis Poulenc figured prominently. Nadia had made his acquaintance about twelve years before, and she appreciated his music (although he had not worked with her). She had already included his works in the programs she had recorded a few weeks earlier for the London radio broadcasts. Before this double departure, Poulenc had written to her from his house in the valley of the Loire:

Dear Nadia,

I hope that before you leave you've got all the Poulenc stuff you need. You know that I am very touched that you like my music a little. That raises my spirits when I'm going through times like these and I spend the whole day loathing myself.

I work at my piano to distract myself, and I'm grateful to God for giving me a taste for other people's music, so that, thanks to the heaps of it piled up on my desk, I can manage to forget my own. Please keep all this in confidence: it would give too much pleasure to those who already don't like me. I know that we should never show any sign of weakness, but with a friend like you I just can't bear to lie. When you get back from London, I'll send the proofs of the Nazelles to you for your approval before having them run off. I'm counting on you to smooth over the rough spots.

Hurriedly, and very affectionately,

Your old Francis

Tell me, once and for all, what I ought to change—I almost always agree with you, and when a "do dièze" like the one in my first children's chorus is left in, in spite of you, just charge it up to my bad taste.

Tell the dear Princess that the concerto* is not a myth, that I'm ashamed, but that I won't turn it over to her until it is as perfect as my imperfect perfection can make it.

The high point of the 1938 American tour was undoubtedly the concert which, thanks to Serge Koussevitsky, Nadia gave in Boston on February 19, at the head of the Boston Symphony Orchestra. Once again, she was the first woman to conduct this orchestra, instantly winning their respect.

She began the initial rehearsal with the Fauré *Requiem*, first running through it without stopping, in a flat, one-dimensional "reading." Next, in a few phrases, she explained to the musicians each part of the work, and then the genesis of the entire

---

*His organ concerto.

95

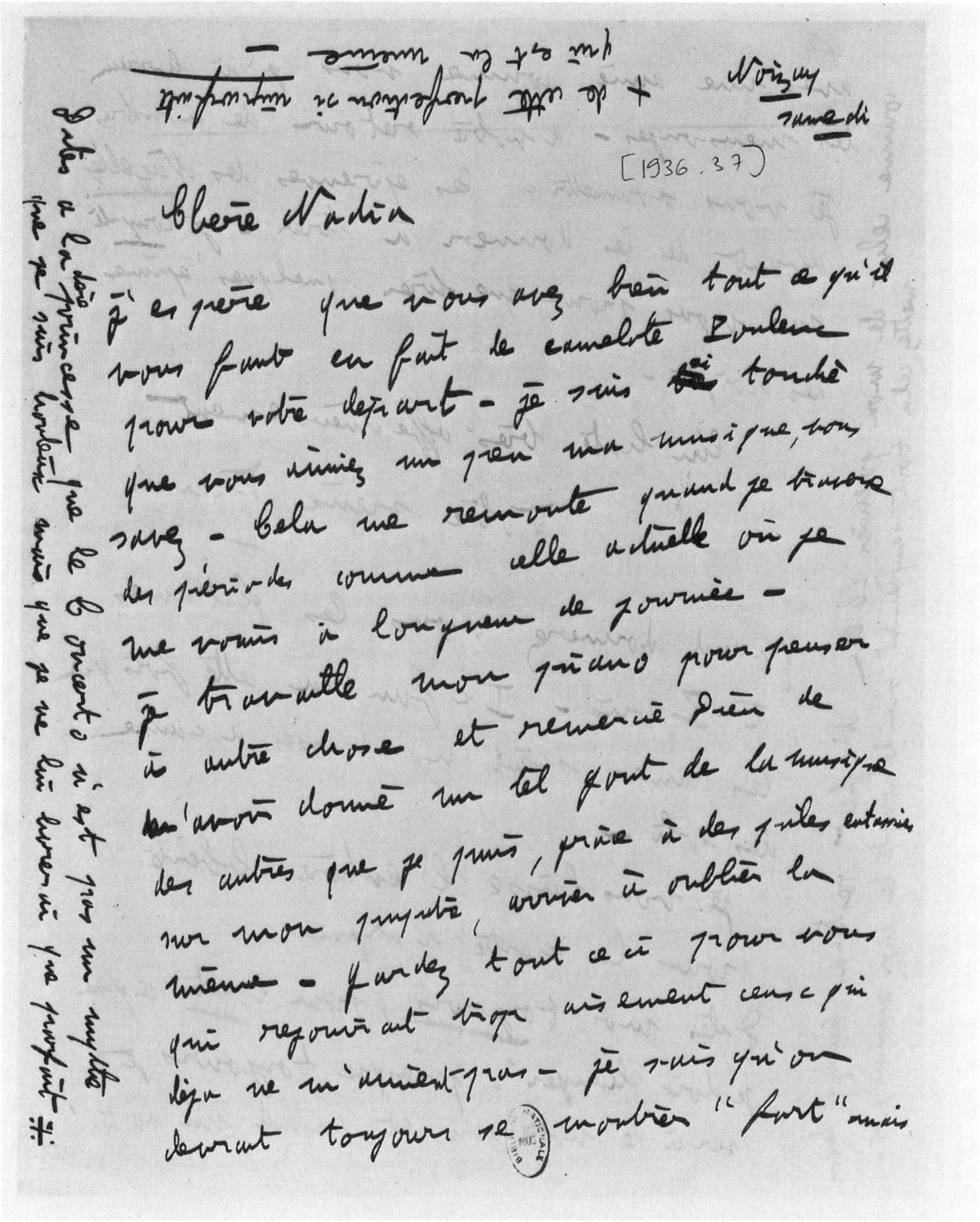

Noizay
samedi

[1936.37]

Chère Nadia

J'espère que vous avez bien tout ce qu'il vous faut en fait de camelote Poulenc pour votre départ — Je suis si touché que vous aimiez un peu ma musique, vous savez — Cela me remonte quand je traverse des périodes comme celle actuelle où je ne vous à longueur de journée —

Je travaille mon piano pour penser à autre chose et remercie Dieu de m'avoir donné un tel goût de la musique des autres que je puis, grâce à des gens entiers sur mon sujet, arriver à oublier la mienne — Gardez tout ceci pour vous qui rejoint trop aisément ceux qui déjà ne m'aiment pas — Je sais qu'on devrait toujours se montrer "fort" mais

[margin, left side]
J'ai à la Princesse que le 6 mars à vos aussitôt que je suis Lindbone arrivé que je ne lui dirai ni que je suis parfait ✝.

Letter from Francis Poulenc (two pages)

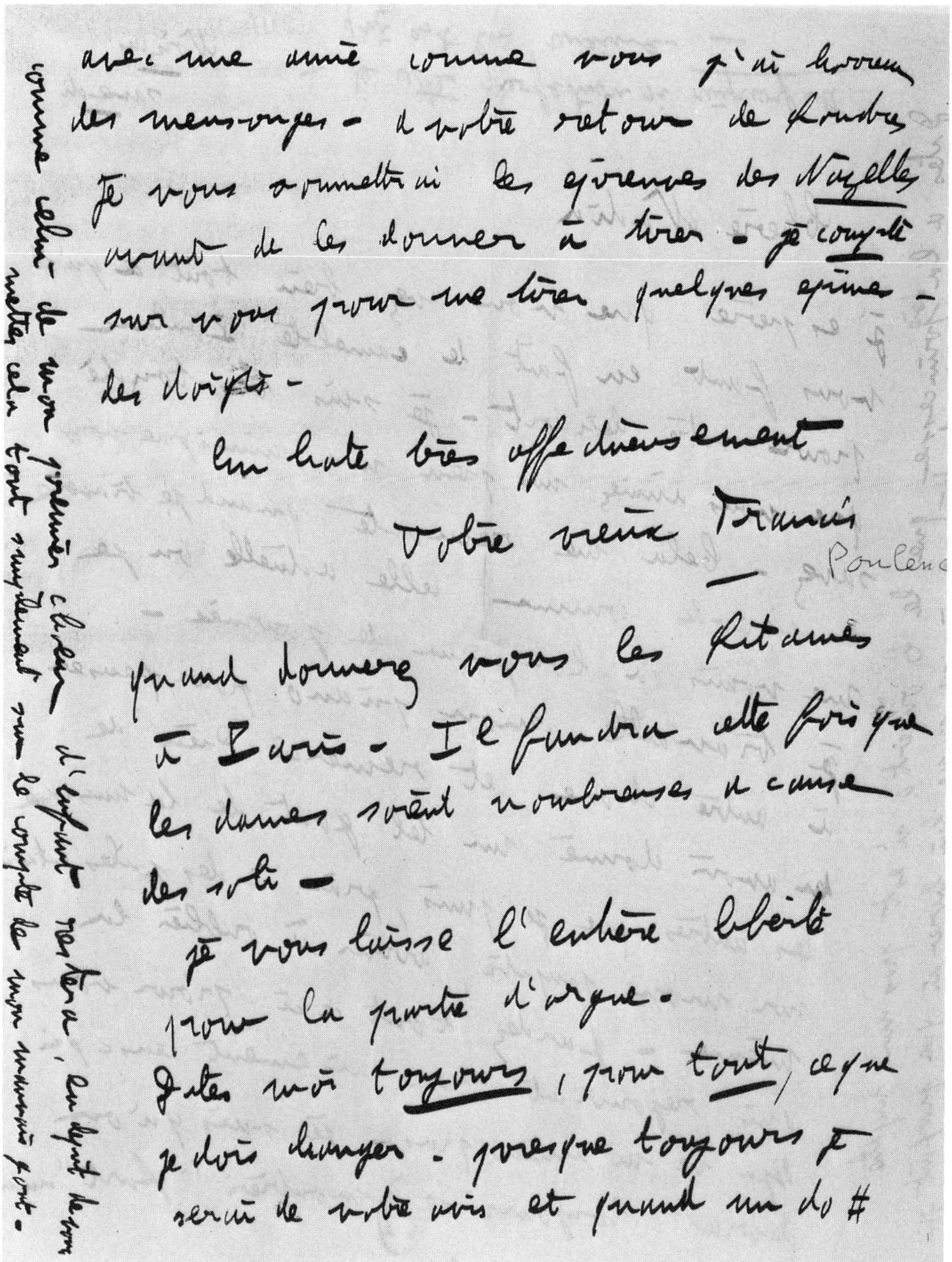

avec une amie comme vous j'ai horreur
des mensonges - A votre retour de Londres
je vous soumettrai les épreuves des Nouvelles
avant de les donner à tirer - je compte
sur vous pour me tirer quelques épines -
des doigts -

En hate très affectueusement
Votre vieux Francis
Poulenc

Quand donnerez vous les Litanies
à Paris - Il faudra cette fois que
les dames soient nombreuses à cause
des soli -

Je vous laisse l'entière liberté
pour la partie d'orgue.

Dites moi toujours, pour tout, ce que
je dois changer - presque toujours je
serai de votre avis et quand un do #

comme celui de mon premier cahier restera, en dépit de son
mettez cela tout simplement sur le compte de mon mauvais goût -

Rehearsal of the Fauré *Requiem* with the Boston Symphony Orchestra, Boston (1938)

work: the clarity, precision, and intelligence of her remarks won over the musicians—and in an instant the whole atmosphere was changed. When they replayed the *Requiem*, the orchestra gave her the exact interpretation she wanted. On the day of the concert, she was rewarded: Fauré's *Requiem* was a veritable triumph.

In fact the whole tour was a success, including the first public performance (at Cambridge) of extracts from the *Diable boiteux* by Jean Françaix, with Hugues Cuenod and Doda Conrad, for whom this little *opéra-comique* was written; and, above all, the first performance on May 8 at the Bliss residence in Dumbarton Oaks of the concerto of the same name by Stravinsky, which Nadia had the great pleasure of being the first to conduct before a small but select audience.

During that trip she became better acquainted with many people she had met the year before. Among them a young woman from a wealthy family of Boston, Winifred Hope Johnstone, who became a very close friend in the years to come, helping her in many ways and even acting as her secretary when Nadia had to stay in the States during the war. Later Winifred Johnstone used to come to Paris regularly for long stays, becoming an habituée if not an actor in the busy life at 36 rue Ballu.

When she left New York after this long and productive stay, she was already thinking of returning. However, this time she did not receive specific invitations for an extended visit to the United States, as she had after her very first trip. Though her concerts were excellently received everywhere, it was nonetheless her classes and her lectures which drew the most fanatically devoted audiences. Her concept of teaching music, her great enthusiasm, her authority, her charisma, set her in a place quite apart where she was virtually unrivaled.

The formidable critic of the *New York Herald Tribune* would not hesitate to write of Nadia Boulanger in February, 1939: "One can already say of her, in the full maturity of her career, that she has enriched her time."

All this was equally true in France: despite the fact that young Olivier Messiaen, appointed to the faculty of the Ecole Normale and working side by side with Nadia,

Nadia Boulanger listens while being introduced to the audience at one of her concerts in the United States in 1939. At the front, her vocal ensemble: from left to right, Marie-Blanche de Polignac, Gisèle Peyron, Irène Kedroff, Nathalie Kedroff, Doda Conrad, and Hugues Cuenod

many years his senior, was beginning to attract a new generation of students, his growing popularity posed no threat to her at this time. (It was he who founded in 1936 the group *Young France*, along with André Jolivet, Daniel Lesur and Yves Baudrier.) In these years when everyone sensed disaster approaching, this woman in her fifties who seemed made of steel continued to exert an ever-growing influence: even her adversaries—and she had some—had to acknowledge the unique place she held, thanks to her exceptional pedagogical gifts, enhanced by her cultural background, her unmatched skill at sight-reading music, and her disconcerting ease at the keyboard.

At the close of 1938, she gave five public lectures in Paris on the history of music which were enormously successful: the subjects included the cantatas of Bach, the songs of Schubert, the mazurkas of Chopin, Fauré's *La bonne chanson*, the "modern authors." The instant they were over, in January 1939, she sailed again for the United States accompanied by Marie-Blanche de Polignac. The rest of the vocal ensemble soon followed, accompanied by Annette Dieudonné, who would also teach a course in solfège at Cambridge.

Boston, March 6, 1939, after the concert given for the benefit of the Lili Boulanger Memorial Fund. From left to right: Walter Piston, John Carpenter, Nadia Boulanger, Roy Harris, Serge Koussevitzky, Mr. Balakovic, Mme. Daniels, Jean Françaix, Edward Hill

This time there were almost four months of concerts, lectures (about fifty), classes, radio broadcasts, social events, interviews, and multiple commitments which she faced without flinching. She was at the same time forging true friendships. The only thing that irritated her was the importance some people attached to her sex: "Let's forget about the fact that I'm a woman," she would interrupt them dryly, "let us talk about music!"

This time it was the New York Philharmonic Orchestra that she conducted (the first woman to do so) on February 11, 1939, in Carnegie Hall. It was completely sold out. On this occasion she returned to her original vocation as a performer: after conducting Jean Françaix in his *Concerto pour piano*, she handed over the baton to John Barbirolli, and rejoined her young protegé in a performance of Mozart's *Concerto for two pianos*. Then she switched to the organ to perform Lili's *Pour les funérailles d'un soldat*, concluding with the madrigals of Monteverdi by her vocal ensemble under her baton.

She was also the first woman to direct the Philadelphia Orchestra, and the American press, like the orchestra players, bowed down before her: "The prejudice against women conductors, which lurks in the bosom of every orchestra player, breaks down instantly when it comes in contact with Mlle. Boulanger's masterful touch."

She made good use of this unprecedented publicity to establish in Boston on March 6, 1939, a Lili Boulanger Memorial Fund dedicated to keeping the memory and the work of her sister alive.

Although there had been a coolness the preceding year between Nadia and Aunt Winnie (who was very hurt by it, but unable to get Nadia to indicate exactly what was troubling her), a letter from the Princess was waiting for her even before she got off the boat at le Havre on July 3, 1939:

> *Dear Nadia,*
>
> *I'm sending you this note which will reach you on board the Normandie, I hope, as soon as you see the shores of France, to tell you how glad I'll be to see you again.*
>
> *The evening of July 3 our friend Lipatti is giving a concert at my place at 10:30 at night, with an orchestra directed by Münch. It would be marvelous if you could come! even late, it would make us so happy. I'm hoping that you won't be too tired, and that you will make the effort and make our joy complete.*
>
> *A thousand loving thoughts*
>
> *W.*

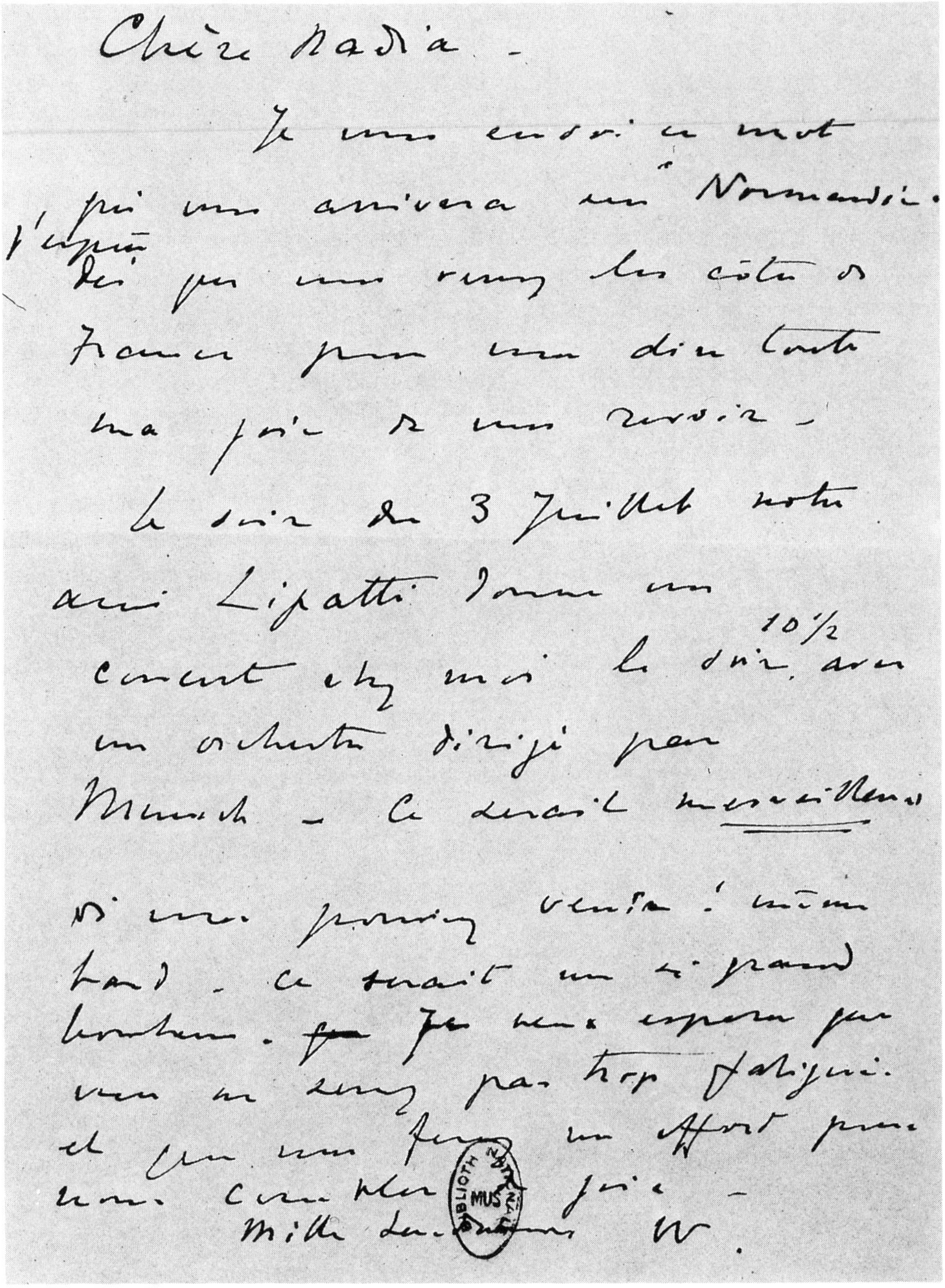

Chère Nadia -

Je vous envoie ce mot qui vous arrivera en Normandie. J'espère dès que vous reviendrez les côtes de France pour vous dire toute ma joie de vous revoir -

Le soir du 3 Juillet notre ami Lipatti donne un concert chez moi le soir, 10½ avec un orchestre dirigé par Munch - Ce serait merveilleux si vous pourriez venir! même tard. Ce serait un si grand bonheur. Je veux espérer que vous ne serez pas trop fatiguée. et que vous ferez un effort pour nous combler de joie -

Mille tendresses W.

Letter from Aunt Winnie

Rue Ballu just before the war in 1939, with Marcelle de Manziarly, Francis Poulenc, Walter Damrosch, Jean Françaix, Marcel Delannoy

This great friendship, which meant so much to Nadia, was definitively disrupted by the war, which broke out in September: the Princess de Polignac was in London and her friends urged her to stay there rather than to return to Paris.

So it was in London, far from all that made her life worthwhile, enduring an unbearable exile, and obliged to get accustomed to the constant bombing (she who used to be petrified at a rumble of thunder) that the Princess de Polignac passed away in the early hours of November 26, 1943, at the beginning of her eightieth year. It was nine months before the liberation of Paris, the city she had so much loved. In "her" country. . . .

Until the end she wrote to Nadia, whom she was not to see again, letters full of both despair and resignation, and a deep affection that outweighed both her sadness and her fear.

> *The collapse of our country . . . has truly been for me a "death in life" . . . that weighs on me so heavily that I don't think I can stand it for very long. I'm too worn out, too old . . . Dear Nadia, I don't think we'll ever recover together our life of other days, but although we are separated, you in Cambridge, and I here, we are held together by so many different chords, by a Bach chorale which in an instant restores the past. . . .*

> *I have lost hope. I cherish in my heart the memory of the beautiful hours I owe you—I keep this memory in the depths of my heart—but I have lost hope of ever seeing you again. Farewell, dear, dear Nadia.*

> *I embrace you tenderly.*

Nadia too found out what it was like to be in exile.

When Fontainebleau was hastily closed at the end of August, 1939, she went to Gargenville, where Stravinsky, who had just lost, one right after the other, his mother, his wife, and his oldest daughter, joined her. They shared weeks of anguish, which frequent visits from Paul Valéry, who lived nearby, made more bearable.

Nadia urged Stravinsky to leave for America, although he had become a French citizen in 1936. It is true that, largely owing to Nadia Boulanger's efforts, he had been named "Norton lecturer" at Harvard, where he was expected at the beginning of the fall semester: ". . . for me, it's a matter of capital importance, because I know what you will do for them—and especially the peace it will afford you for your work . . ." she had written to him in May, 1939, from Cambridge, upon learning of his appointment.

So Stravinsky made up his mind to take on his new position without any further delay, taking with him his friend Vera, whom he was soon to marry.

Mobilization decimated the ranks of Nadia's pupils, and caught many of her friends. Among them was Francis Poulenc, whose Concerto for organ, which he had finally finished, she had premiered a few months earlier in the salon of the Princess. He wrote to her:

> *Let me hear from you. I must tell you right now that there is a letter addressed to you in case something should happen to me. It will give you a lot of tasks, but who could do a better job of them than you?*

> *There is so much that I wanted to do better in music—I was about to begin, I think. I had figured out what it meant to be forty years old, and I was discounting my ten best years. If God lends me life, perhaps I'll still be able to sneak in a few good ones. It is sad to think that the other war considerably hobbled my musical education, and that this one*

In 1940, before her exile to the United States

is playing the same trick on me all over again. I wouldn't write that to anyone else, for in such hours as these they might think this a matter of very slight interest. Think of me, and write me letters full of stories.

I kiss you tenderly.

Francis

Nadia spent the "phony war" in Paris. General Huntziger enlisted her services to give a few concerts to the armed forces, either conducting an orchestra of mobilized musicians, or taking with her an improvised vocal group (Cuenod was in Switzerland, Conrad on tour in Asia with the pianist Lili Kraus . . .). After one of these concerts near Sedan, she wrote: "You cannot imagine all those men in uniform, some just back from the front . . . Debussy's *Dieu, qu'il la fait bon regarder* was listened to in the most profound silence."

Just before Christmas, 1939, at the head of the orchestra of the Société des Concerts of the Conservatoire, in the concert room of the Conservatoire in Paris, she conducted a memorable performance of Carissimi's oratorio, *Jephté*.

When Belgium was invaded in the spring of 1940, she was in Lausanne, where she had given several lectures during the winter (Paderewski came to pay her homage during one of them). Without finishing her classes at the Conservatoire, she left Lausanne hurriedly to get back to Paris . . . and soon found herself at the wheel of her car, fleeing the German army along roads swarming with bewildered refugees.

She arrived without incident at Uzerches, in Corrèze, where her old friends, the Loudons (whose daughter married a wealthy American, Arthur Sachs) had an estate. It was there that she learned that France had surrendered. And it was there that, as early as the month of July, she decided to leave for the United States.

In order to get the indispensable exit visa from the Vichy government, she requested a legal and binding contract which the Longy School of Music of Cambridge, Massachusetts, sent her immediately.

After a hazardous journey across Spain in the company of an American woman friend who was returning home, and a long wait for a boat in Lisbon which was packed with people trying to leave, she finally sailed on the American liner *Excambion*, at the same time as Paderewski. She arrived in New York on December 6, 1940; once again, the Damrosch family was there to welcome her.

This decision to flee from France was surprising in more than one respect. In the first place, although Nadia Boulanger was authoritarian by nature, she was, paradoxically, indecision itself: once her mind was made up, there was no changing it, but most of the time she put off committing herself until the last possible moment, and did so only when the pressure of time or events left her no alternative. But in this case she apparently had not the slightest hesitation.

Yet this decision ran counter both to her independent character and to her constant concern for her dignity, to say nothing of her slightly chauvinistic patriotism; we will probably never know the underlying reasons that motivated it.

In 1941, Nadia Boulanger rejoins some of her friends from whom she had been separated eighteen months earlier. Here with, from left to right, Mrs. Cameron, Mrs. Duncan McDuffie, Mrs. John F. Forbes (seated)

Officially it was a matter of honoring the engagements to which she had committed herself the preceding year: but this is hardly convincing, especially in view of the fact that, years later, Nadia Boulanger did not hesitate to cancel all her American contracts at the last moment upon learning that Hélène Détroyat, the granddaughter of her former guardian, Williams Bouwens, was on her deathbed, victim of an accident in London. A catastrophe of such magnitude for France as that of 1940 would nonetheless seem a reason at least as valid for someone who never let herself be governed solely by personal feelings.

One can readily believe that she was not in the least concerned about having to deal with the Germans, whom she detested. But she always expressed a lively admiration for Marshal Pétain, whose conduct she would never, even for a moment, discuss. At that time, besides, she made no secret of the fact that she endorsed the positions taken by the Action Française, including that of antisemitism, which she herself vigorously espoused—or at any rate gave lip-service to (although she never applied the slightest racial criterions where her students were concerned). She was even not entirely averse to dictatorship and dictators, if only because of her love for order: "Given the opportunity, who would not be a dictator?" she asked reasonably enough, adding immediately, "In music, I myself am a dictator!" In music only? . . . It is surely not entirely inappropriate that the series of radio broadcasts devoted to her just before the war by the BBC was entitled "The Tender Tyrant"—an epithet which one of her pupils, Alan Kendall, would pick up some forty years later to use as the title of his book on Nadia Boulanger.

Did she simply obey a sort of impulse to go where she could be near Stravinsky, for whom she felt a sort of passionate affection beyond reason, and whose departure for the United States, which she had very strongly recommended, had left an unbearable void in her life? Did she perhaps, without being consciously aware of it, entertain other hopes for the future?

But that takes us into the realm of pure speculation. What is certain is that, after having with vigorous determination managed to get herself to the United States, she went into a profound depression, caused by, in her own words, feelings of remorse and shame.

The March anniversaries were terribly painful times for her; twenty-three years after the death of Lili, six years after the death of her mother, she wrote to her "dear Igor" . . . "the impossibility of doing here what we always used to do in Paris . . . The feeling of shame for having left at such a moment has taken on sorrowful dimensions in my mind."

She wrote in the same vein to Doda Conrad, with whom she had been joyfully reunited in New York, where he landed after his tour in the Orient; the words appear somewhat enigmatic: "As for me, I drag about with me the shame of having left (there was nothing else for me to do, I know, but that doesn't make the least bit of difference). I carry the old, open wounds that I despair of having healed: they are all I have left of a past so sweet, so dear, and so beautiful, and if it were a question of making the right choice, I believe my decision would be made without hesitation."

However, she received a letter from Cannes written by Marcelle de Manziarly which must have brought her some comfort, since it informed her that Annette Dieudonné was back in Paris and would, on March 15, 1941, "have a mass said at Trinity Church, without music, due to the present circumstances." Dieudonné had made the trip to Gargenville and asked Marcelle to tell Mademoiselle Boulanger also "that there is naturally, a lot of disorder after those who were living there left, but that much is now safe: the old plates, and the carpets as well, and part of the linen, the bedcovers, the silver, the music—the papers—Madame Boulanger's little coffee pot, Madame Bouwens' milk pitcher, lots of knick-knacks—and that everything is going well and is perfectly normal at the rue Ballu."

Over and above her classes in harmony, counterpoint, fugue, and composition at Longy, Nadia Boulanger resumed her activities as lecturer, conductor, and even soloist, mostly in New England. And she took part also in the benefit organized by Doda Conrad on behalf of Polish refugees (he was of Polish origin himself); and on April 5, 1941, at Carnegie Hall, she conducted at a gala concert in honor of Paderewski, who was very much admired, but who was then ill, and would die two months later in New York.

These multiple activities, together with the depressing thoughts that obsessed her, left her exhausted: she accepted an invitation from the Dominican Convent at Santa Clara, in Wisconsin, to come there for a six weeks rest. Six weeks during which she gave classes to the sisters! These were appreciated so much that her study-sojourns there became a regular activity.

But this time she had taken on too much. En route to California in August, 1941, she wrote to Stravinsky to let him know of her arrival:

> *Dear friend,*
> *I will be in Santa Barbara Monday—but to have a complete rest for at least ten days. I have just finished my classes at the Convent and . . . I have no choice. It's nothing, and is of no importance. But a tired old heart just can't stand the burden of remorse—on top of the everyday effort—and I just can't become reconciled to the idea that I left everyone over there, suffering the way they are suffering. . . .*

At Santa Barbara, she stayed with her friends the Sachses, whom she had run into again in America, where they had returned after leaving their relatives in Uzerches. Thanks to the friendly atmosphere, she recovered rapidly, happy to be surrounded by many other friends, the Blisses, and Richard Hammond, and especially Stravinsky; so happy, that she prolonged her stay until right up to the time she had to return to the Longy School in October.

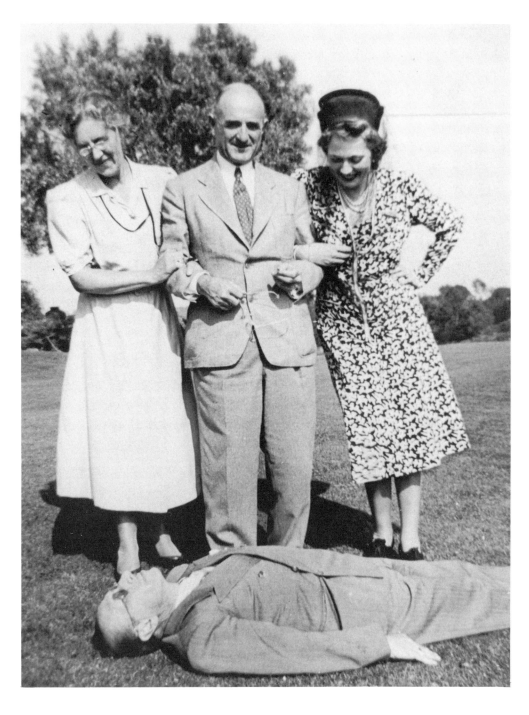

Santa Barbara, August 1941: watching Stravinsky play dead are his new wife, Vera, Arthur Sachs, and Nadia

There she recreated her "Wednesdays," focusing on Bach's Cantatas; she was particularly insistent about sight-reading, a skill somewhat neglected in American music schools at that time. Those trained by her had distinct advantages over their fellow students, which also serves to explain the success of her classes.

In the spring of 1942, in addition, she accepted an offer from the Peabody Conservatory, and from then on went to Baltimore once a week to give classes in the history of music and orchestration, besides classes in harmony, counterpoint, fugue and composition.

Once again, she was ceaselessly working, as though she didn't want to allow her mind to have a single moment of repose. From Edgewood College (another Dominican convent in Madison, Wisconsin, where she spent the summer of 1942, ostensibly resting and relaxing), she wrote to Stravinsky, who had finally settled down in Santa Barbara with Vera:

> How much I miss Vera and you. Your presence is so necessary for my heart and mind—but, alas, California is far away.
>
> Saint-Exupéry has been a great help—he is so reliable, so good—but he's leaving any day now to rejoin Giraud, and now has found an inner tranquility, since he is going to get into the action at last.
>
> Forgive me for not having corrected the sonata yet—if you only knew what my life is like, you would understand. I'll get busy with it, I promise. . . .

This sonata was the one for two pianos which she had the pleasure of presenting to the public for the first time in a concert at Edgewood College; her partner was one of her own students, Richard Johnson.

But she was not the only one who deeply felt the misfortunes and the doubts of all those newly displaced people, who tried to comfort one another. Even Stravinsky, who didn't have the reputation of being especially sensitive in matters of emotion, did not escape these attacks of melancholy. He wrote to Nadia: "Because you are there, it seems to me the path is less dark."

At the end of the academic year in 1943, she was so exhausted with overwork, that she was obliged to obey her doctor's order to get some rest—but seriously, this time. The Sachses provided her with a little house in Santa Barbara: the California climate, the presence of attentive friends, the constant neighborly interchange with Stravinsky, rapidly restored her strength and composure.

These months spent in California constituted a genuine pause, the only one, it seems, in the permanent whirlwind that her life had been and was soon to be again. This period of rest, actually only a relative one, allowed her to pursue her own work,

Study-vacation in 1942 at the Dominican convent in Santa Clara

but that did not prevent her from welcoming certain of her students who came to work with her. Doubtless at this quiet time, as never before, she had more leisure than usual to ponder the fundamental questions of existence, which in her case meant problems of conscience and matters of a religious nature above all.

Toward the end of her life she would confide: "Only within the confines of the cloister would I have had some chance of doing successfully what I would have liked to accomplish. I did not have the strength for that, and the cloistered life didn't appeal to me. Yet my life was not so very far from that, restricted as it was within rather narrow bounds, but without allowing me the privilege of consecrating myself wholly to what is most essential and subordinating all the rest of that."

To make her life even easier, her friends, the Sachses, gave her a Chevrolet coupé at Christmas. She kept it for her entire stay in the States, giving it to Stravinsky when she left.

At that time everything in the United States was focused on the war raging in Europe and the Pacific. Nadia was effectively cut off from news of France, and she was still in California when she learned of the allied invasion of Normandy on June 6, 1944, and then of the liberation of Paris on August 25. Her emotion, her pangs of regret at being so far away, can readily be imagined.

Santa Barbara, 1943: solitude, and at work with Stravinsky

Hope was reborn, but indirect news from France that those close to her were safe did not reach her until the beginning of winter (when she was giving a joint recital with Stravinsky at Mills College, where Darius Milhaud taught). But when Nadia was finally able to return to France there were many empty places in her life: Saint-Exupéry had disappeared somewhere over the Mediterranean at the controls of his plane; Princess de Polignac was no more; Paul Valéry had survived the occupation and the liberation unscathed only to die, world-weary, on July 24, 1945. A whole epoch, a whole civilized way of life, had disappeared forever.

Nadia Boulanger got her exit visa from the United States a few days before the capitulation of Germany on May 8, 1945, but military personnel had first claim on transatlantic transport, besides which the war against Japan was still going on and would not end until more than three months later.

To make the waiting time pass more quickly, and to feel closer to Europe, she went back to Boston in September, 1945, and for one more trimester taught at Longy, all the while inundating her friends in France with packages which must have seemed to them like a shower of gifts from a fairytale heaven.

Nadia Boulanger found herself once again also at the head of the Boston Symphony Orchestra, conducting it twice during a series of concerts celebrating the hundredth anniversary of the birth of Gabriel Fauré—a composer whose works she had largely introduced to North America. She conducted a concert version of *Pénélope*, and, of course, the *Requiem*, which she later repeated in Potsdam, New York, only a few days before she set sail, on January 3, 1946, on a barely modified troop ship bound for Europe. Until the very last moment she was surrounded by a group of friends whose loyalty had never flagged during the five years of her stay—even though a few of them had backed off a little from time to time, for Mademoiselle Boulanger was not always the easiest person to get along with!

Shortly before she sailed, she had received a letter—typed, as usual—from Stravinsky, who had decided not only to remain in the United States, but to give up his recently acquired French citizenship as well, in order to become an American:

> *Nadia dear, you too? Too bad. So you are really sailing in December. . . .*
>
> *Details, please, about your appointment to the Paris Conservatory. . . . Professor of Accompaniment! What does that title mean?*
>
> *Even if it is only very brief, I insist on some news of what you are doing. . . .*
>
> *How can I thank you enough for your car? It's been here at our place for a week. Vera really needs it desperately and your gift will be a great help to her when she has errands to run, and also when our Dodge is in the shop. . . .*

With Stravinsky at Mills College in October 1944 visiting the home of Darius and Madeleine Milhaud. Below: Boston, October 1945: shortly before her return to France, in the company of Serge Koussevitzky and Aaron Copland.

It was true that, thirty-five years after her first unsuccessful candidacy, Nadia Boulanger had finally been appointed to the faculty of the Conservatoire without even having to apply: her old friend Claude Delvincourt had proposed her for the post. Delvincourt had guided the Conservatoire through all the hazards of the occupation with superb skill, protecting his pupils with wisdom and courage.

The letter in which Delvincourt confirmed her appointment had nothing extraordinary about it except for its postscript, indicative of the problems and preoccupations of the French, emerging painfully from four years of nightmare:

November 22, 1945

My dear Nadia,

Since I sent you the telegram announcing the good news, I haven't had a moment to pick up my pen and tell you—along with my sincere congratulations— how happy I am at the thought of seeing you come into a house that holds so many old memories for both of us.

I'm dictating this letter because I'm so rushed that it's impossible for me to pick up the pen myself, and I want to express my very hearty thanks to you for the magnificent package (the third) which arrived in perfect condition.

Thank you again with all my heart. I look forward to seeing you soon. In the meantime, please accept my most affectionate regards.

The Director of the Conservatoire
Claude Delvincourt

P.S. You're doubtless going to think me very bold, but since I hope to see you next month, could you possibly slip into your baggage a little item which is unavailable at this moment in France: I'm talking about springs for the mechanism that closes the main door of the Conservatoire. It's not working properly: the door stays open all day long, sending cold drafts through the house, and everything could be put to rights if we had the springs in question. If you can make this little purchase for me, you'll be reimbursed as soon as you get here. Thank you once again.

The gadget is a Yale reversible, #75.

C.D.

When she disembarked on January 17, 1946, at La Pallice (uneasy about what sort of a welcome might be awaiting her, for she was still tortured with remorse at having left in 1940) Nadia Boulanger suddenly came face to face with the harsh realities of that country's day to day existence, which she could never have imagined from her sheltered life in far-away America. Having just left the land of abundance which America had continued to be in spite of the war, she found herself plunged into a gaunt France still in want of everything from salt and sugar to gas and cars, to say nothing of paper, heat, clothes . . . and springs for door stops!

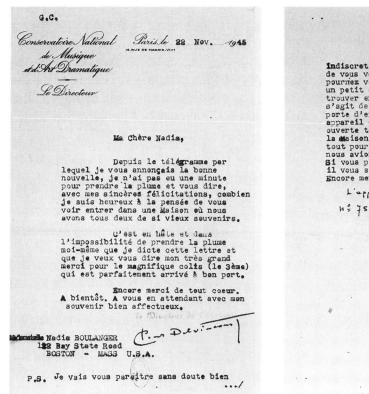

Letter from Claude Delvincourt

She herself had not changed very much, except for one notable detail; shortly after she had arrived in America, she had traded her pince-nez for glasses, which made her face somewhat less severe.

Her return was triumphal. It took place under privileged material conditions: Doda Conrad—who had joined the American army in 1942 and was now in France—was waiting for her at the foot of the gangplank with a car; Annette Dieudonné and Jean Françaix were with him. He drove them to Paris after an overnight stop at LeMans.

She found the rue Ballu apartment intact: Annette Dieudonné had been living there since the beginning of the occupation to protect it against possible requisition. She managed to do so, just as she succeeded, at the Bibliothèque du Conservatoire, where she had arranged to have herself appointed after Mademoiselle Boulanger left, in keeping the most precious of its manuscripts out of the hands of the Germans. Her Legion of Honor attests to this.

When the initial burst of emotion, relief, and effusive interchange (never excessive on Nadia Boulanger's part) was over with, and after another welcome-home reception which brought all the friends together again on February 4, life on the rue Ballu quickly assumed the rhythm of former days, as though, once the American experience was placed between parentheses, nothing had changed. Now that Nadia was back again, the funeral mass in the month of March at the Trinity took on symbolic overtones.

Everything fell back into its accustomed place: the private lessons, the Wednesday courses (attended, according to Cuenod who put in an appearance there only rarely, by an "incredible circle of incredible ladies"), the concerts, the lectures—and even the Fontainebleau School.

Thanks to the generosity of a host of benefactors, most of whom were American, the Fontainebleau School was actually able to open its doors half-way as early as the summer of 1946 . . . with a total enrollment of only ten, all of whom initially signed up for piano. But Nadia Boulanger offered them a class once a week in July—and, when it proved successful, twice a week in August. While she was still in America, Nadia had suggested to Damrosch that he appoint the cellist Paul Bazelaire director of the school; Robert Casadesus was chosen instead: he too had returned from the United States where he had gone off to wait out the war. While there, he had even tried to recreate a sort of Fontainebleau in exile, an effort which did not have Nadia Boulanger's approval.

But the major new event for her was quite clearly her class at the Conservatoire: "l'accompagnement au piano" gave her the opportunity to introduce into that bastion of tradition her own teaching methods, which had not changed, and to tackle everything that had anything to do with music.

Almost all her pupils took private lessons with her, and attended the Wednesday sessions. She was explicit about these two aspects of teaching, which to her were essential: "Not to see the students individually would be to do them an irreparable injustice, but, on the other hand, it is humanly if not musically essential to give them a group feeling, the opportunity to agree or to disagree, and to find out what the others think."

Once again, pupils flocked to her: she was still unique . . . but she was no longer the only one. In 1942, Olivier Messiaen, freed from prisoner-of-war camp, was appointed to teach harmony at the Conservatoire: and a new cult came into being which would draw an increasing number of adherents. And there is no doubt that Nadia must have been saddened when, in 1947, Delvincourt created a class in analysis

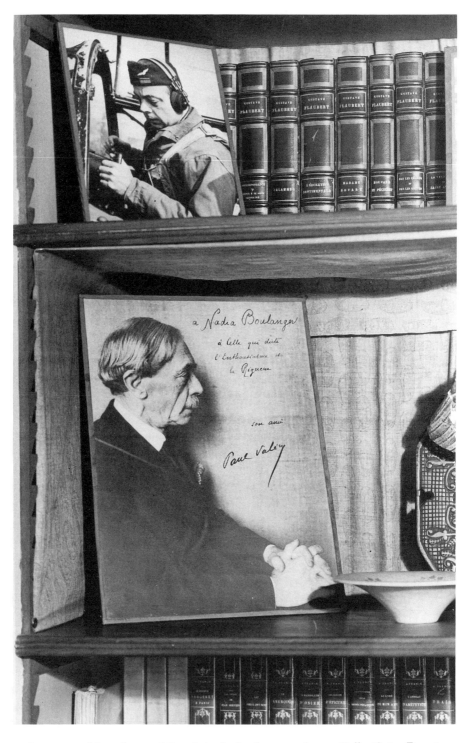

Souvenirs of dear departed friends in the bookcase at the rue Ballu (Saint-Exupéry and Paul Valéry)

and music appreciation especially for him: in other days would she not have been the one rightly entitled to it?

That year, 1947, was the very year in which she celebrated her sixtieth birthday, and on that occasion Stravinsky wrote a "Petit Canon" for her. That same year Messiaen was just turning forty. Nadia could do nothing about the generation gap which separated them. Certainly she was as much as ever fully the master of her science, and as capable as ever of dispensing all the energy necessary to transmit it, just as she had been doing for forty years, with her keen intelligence and that authority which no one dared challenge.

But with the passage of the years she could not escape the inviolable law: for a teacher, the moment inevitably comes when, no matter how "modern" one may have been, or how dynamic one still appears to be, one's teaching little by little loses spontaneity. Nothing can prevent this: what was once a matter of constant innovation gradually becomes more or less repetitive. It is no longer the "Great Adventure" itself, but simply a re-run of the film about the "Great Adventure."

The phenomenon takes its time about showing up, but a very long life always makes it inescapable. And so it was for Nadia Boulanger: and so it is now for Olivier Messiaen; and so it will be tomorrow for Pierre Boulez—and so also for all those who pick up the torch in the future, holding it high and bright in the beginning, but inevitably letting it flicker before it is snatched away from them in turn. Ad infinitum. . . .

Even were she aware that things were in process of changing, Nadia had scarcely time to be concerned about it. The Cercle Interallié concerts had begun again towards the end of 1946; beginning the following year the *Club d'Essai de la Radio* called upon her several times a year; she gave frequent concerts in London (where she also recorded programs for the BBC), as well as in Holland, in Italy and in Switzerland. There she had the good fortune to run into Dino Lipatti, who had escaped from Rumania in 1943 with the woman who was later to become his wife, Madeleine Cantacuzène. From Italy she brought back with her a domestic couple, Zita and Giuseppe, who remained in her service from then on; she would assume the responsibility of seeing to the education of their two sons. And then she went to Monaco where Prince Pierre had officially appointed her *Maître de chappelle* in 1947. And, of course, when she was in Paris, she never missed an important concert, especially when the performers bore such names as Bernstein, Milstein, Menuhin, Enesco, Schnabel, Lipatti, Milhaud, Magaloff, Curzon, etc.—or, naturally, when her own pupils were participating.

A gift from Stravinsky for Nadia Boulanger's sixtieth birthday

121

The examining jury for singing at Fontainebleau in 1950. From left to right: Jean Françaix, Nicolas Nabokov, Nadia Boulanger, Jean-Pierre Alaux, Jean Périer, Marcel Dupré, Germaine Martinelli

She was in demand everywhere for concerts, lectures, classes, and also for competition juries. In 1949, the year before she was made director of the Music School at Fontainebleau, succeeding Robert Casadesus, who had resigned from the post, she served on the jury of the Concours Long-Thibaud, the first of a long series of such juries which would take her over the course of twenty years to the four corners of Europe. Marcel Dupré would continue another three years at the head of the entire Fontainebleau School, but when he retired in 1953, it was Nadia Boulanger who took his place. From that moment on—for twenty-six summers—she held undivided sway over that institution.

Similarly, she reigned undisputed over the somewhat reduced musical activities of the Singer-Polignac Foundation, created in the Princess' will contingent upon Nadia's assuming its direction. The first concert took place on June 21, 1951, in the drawing-rooms of the mansion on the rue Cortambert. Even stripped of its furnishings, paintings, and collections, and despite its bare walls, the house preserved the spirit of the woman who had built it and who had animated it for nearly four decades. The program was typical of Nadia Boulanger: it went from Claudin de Sermisy to Georges Enesco and Jean-Michel Defaÿ (one of Nadia's pupils, only eighteen years old) and did not fail to include, en route, Berlioz and Fauré.

Nadia's vocal ensemble regained some of its former members, Hugues Cuenod, Paul Derenne, Doda Conrad; but new names appeared as the need arose: for several years the Swiss singer Flore Wend served as the main soprano. Marie-Blanche de

Polignac no longer sang; she was soon to fall victim to an illness which would, over the course of a few years, get the better of her courage and her beauty.

Dinu Lipatti was suffering from a similar ailment. Every time she could, Nadia went to see him in Switzerland (he was living in Geneva). In 1950, when an attack of influenza, that left her "in a sorry state," impelled her to spend some time in Montana recuperating, she wrote to Stravinsky from there:

> *Also wanted to see my dear Dinu Lipatti, who is very ill. How you would love his spirit, and the way he plays, and the way he thinks. Alas . . . will he ever get better? He is confined to bed now.*
>
> *. . . and the future looks black for him. He asked me to pay his respects to you, and to thank you. When he utters your name, such an expression of joy lights up his poor face.*

The following month, however, Lipatti was in London, giving concerts and making recordings—"unsuccessful ones," he wrote to her:

July 23, 1950: Allegra Markevitch on the day of her baptism, perched between Nadia Boulanger and Dinu Lipatti

. . . another vertebra is bothering me, to the point where I can scarcely leave my bed. In an hour I'm starting radiotherapy on the trouble spot; it will last not quite four weeks and is guaranteed to correct the problem. In spite of everything, my general state of health is not bad. Approximately two blood transfusions a week . . . But I can't stand being idle . . .

Our most affectionate regards go with you, and our loyal thoughts full of admiration.

Your very devoted,

Dinu

At the end of the month of July he was well enough for the baptism of the first child of Igor Markevitch and his new wife Topazia to take place at his home in Geneva. On June 29 he had written to his "very dear Nadia":

It's all arranged with the Igors . . . it will be intimate, at our place, you will stay with us in our country house, if that's all right with you.

My health is still fine, and Madeleine is radiant with joy. In two days we will start the records, which will be finished on July 13. On the 15th, I'm playing at Berne and then: complete rest.

What a joy it was to have heard you. I embrace you tenderly.

After the "rest," there would be a last recital on September 16 at Besançon, his final appearance in public. Nadia was there (she spent almost the whole month close to him in Geneva). "Not the slightest sign of anguish," he told her, "on the contrary, nothing but the joy of giving."

Nadia left him on September 30: they would not see one another again. On November 24 he sent her a card, the last one:

My dearest Nadia,

I had to be as far gone as I am not to be able to reply to your very affectionate messages. I love you dearly and your thoughts during these past weeks have been a great support to me. I am a long way from having won a victory, but the real danger is far away. On the other hand, my nerves are as low as they can get.

One evening I actually flung myself on the piano, just as you predicted I would do. You know me so well! All my thoughts are with you, and your photo beside my bed helps me over the difficult moments. I embrace you.

Dinu

A week later, on December 2, 1950, Dinu Lipatti, archangel-musician, died at the age of thirty-three. He had written to Nadia two months earlier: "I am happy to have lived on this earth at the same time as you. Thank you for everything you gave

le 24 XI 50

Ma très chère Nadia

Il a fallu que je sois détruit comme je le suis pour ne pas pouvoir répondre à vos messages si affectueux. Je vous aime tendrement et votre pensée de ces dernières semaines a été pour moi un grand soutien. Je suis loin d'avoir vaincu, mais le _vrai_ danger est loin. Par contre les nerfs sont on ne peut plus bas

En effet, un soir je me suis précipité au piano, comme vous l'avez prévu. Vous me connaissez si bien ! Toute ma pensée est près de vous et votre photo près du lit m'aide aux moments difficiles. Je vous embrasse Dinu

The last lines written by Dinu Lipatti to Nadia Boulanger

At the time of the première of *The Rake's Progress* in Venice, dinner with Prince Pierre of Monaco

have lived on this earth at the same time as you. Thank you for everything you gave us." Better than any other, and before all others, Nadia Boulanger had understood what he himself had to give.

Upon hearing of his death, Marcelle de Manziarly wrote Nadia, saying: "You have lost a son, and we have lost a creature of light"—the very expression Madeleine Lipatti would always use when speaking of him. . . . That heart-breaking date would remain graven in Nadia's memory: no need of the little notebook to remind her each year to communicate to Madeleine the grief she so sincerely felt.

No matter how strong the inner pull that drew her toward her memories, Nadia Boulanger had no intention of ignoring the time in which she lived. She took a special interest in the work of Boulez. Accompanying it by a letter in a script so microscopic as to defy reproduction, he sent her one of his compositions, *Visage Nuptial*, "still lacking two poems, not copied out. They are in quarter tone. Even though that is of minor importance, you can at least get a good idea of it."

And since Nadia Boulanger did let him know of her "interest," he replied on March 28, 1951:

> *Dear Mademoiselle,*
>
> *Your letter meant a lot to me. For even if I don't really have to be understood, a certain atmosphere of "understanding" plays a part in the development of one's own tendencies. Perhaps it may even be a determining factor that pushes one toward the discovery of phenomena as yet unexpressed. . . .*

But this new direction in music remained radically alien to her, and after attending one of the first concerts of the "Domaine Musical" in 1954, she wrote to Stravinsky: "The so-called 'modern' works have wrought havoc—for Varèse, violent reactions. How out-of-date and pompous they are! Bah! The tide flows on and sweeps them away . . . leaving not a single trace."

At the end of her life, she made her thoughts very plain: "It seems to me that a lot of people have nothing to say, and they lean on a system just to hide from themselves the fact that they have nothing to say. But no system has ever prevented anyone from expressing himself nor from having genius."

Without a doubt she was then thinking of Stravinsky. With the first production of his opera, *The Rake's Progress*, at the Fenice on September 11, 1951, under his own direction (Nadia, from "the gods," had followed the final rehearsals before attending several performances), Igor Stravinsky made contact, once again, with the Europe he had left behind eleven years earlier. Under the influence of his shadow Robert Craft (an influence which many considered harmful in every respect), Stravinsky was ready to discover dodecaphonic music, and would try his hand at it as early as 1952 with the *Septett* for wind instruments.

This development could not have failed to distress Nadia, even if she felt Stravinsky's personality was strong enough to dominate the system rather than be dominated by it. "Everything works out for him from the moment he finds something in it to build on," she would say later on, as though to justify herself for having absolved him.

While the rehearsals of *The Rake's Progress* in French were underway at the Opéra-Comique where it was to be performed in 1953, and on the very morning of the Paris opening of his *Cantata* for soprano and tenor, Nadia wrote to him:

Judging by the letters that came from Boston, I gather that you were satisfied, dear friend, with the performance.

Here we're working hard—but where it's getting us, I don't really know. Tonight the Cantate. Will it be successful? I'll write and tell you.

The more I read, the more I play this score, the more I like it—no, I loved it right away—but the better I see and understand everything. When one sees the floods of notes in which so many—well, yes—musicians indulge, one can easily understand the sad reason for their apparent richness.

And there you are, just as Mozart was long ago, with only a few notes—but they are the right ones.

A lot of activity everywhere—"much ado about nothing," often—from time to time, a surprise. But I didn't mean to talk to you about aesthetics. I miss you—I'm sad—your presence is so necessary to me. But we are still dedicated to our task—and after all, with all humility, we keep on trying to lead toward the right path. Perhaps that's not so bad for those who can accomplish only so very little!

With a warm embrace for Vera and yourself, I am as ever your

Nadia B.

very best regards to Bob Craft

Stravinsky's first really important serial work would be the *Canticum Sacrum* in 1956. But two years earlier, *In Memoriam Dylan Thomas* clearly established his radical departure from his former aesthetics. Thus he was linked to what Nadia Boulanger always vigorously opposed, namely ways of writing which "dehumanized" musical expression, and which resulted—as they did in the case of Schoenberg—in something considered hermetic. "For music to be understood, one must be able to experience it intellectually and emotionally: either of these factors, by itself, is not enough," she professed.

So, even though we are quite aware that the least note of Stravinsky's had the power to elicit an "emotional" response from her, we are nonetheless surprised to read what she wrote to him on November 7, 1954: "Read 'In memoriam'—what music—everything is there—I would like to talk about each note, but . . . you know these truths better than I do. One grasps in one's hand something real, something concrete, and also one reaches for something that I don't have the bad taste to express. . . ."

These words do not fail to call to mind her famous "you know what I think," uttered with conviction to artists to whom, in actual fact, she did not want to express the unflattering things she thought of their performance; but here the tone seems sincere.

31 mai 1958

Si j'en juge par les lettres reçues de Boston – je suppose
que vous avez été content. Cher Ami, de la représentation.
Ici, on travaille beaucoup – mais où on en est, je l'ignore.
Ce soir, la Cantate. Sera-ce bien ? Je vous écrirai –
Plus je lis cette partition, plus je l'aime – non, je l'ai
aimée tout de suite, mais mieux je lis, j'entends tout.
Quand on voit le débordement de notes auquel se livrent
encore tant de – – enfin, oui, de musiciens, on comprend
bien la triste raison de leur apparente richesse.

Et vous êtes là, comme fut jadis Mozart, avec quelques
notes – mais celles-là sont les vraies.

Grande activité, partout – "beaucoup de bruit pour
rien", souvent – de temps à autre, une surprise.
Mais ce n'est pas d'esthétique que je viens vous parler.
Vous me manquez – je suis triste – votre présence est
une telle nécessité – mais au reste attaché à sa
besogne – et après tout, bien humblement on essaie
de mener vers le bon chemin. Ce n'est peut-être pas
si mal pour ceux qui ne peuvent que si peu !

Je vous embrasse Vera et vous et suis
Toujours votre
mille amitiés à Bob Craft

Letter from Nadia Boulanger to Stravinsky

And, indeed, even though the programs of her classes for all practical purposes failed to include this type of music, she was never to cut herself off from certain composers, like Boulez for instance, whom she sent to Stravinsky in America in 1957. This gave rise to an interesting exchange of letters in April/May of that year.

From Nadia Boulanger to Stravinsky:

> *Boulez spoke to me very seriously about his stay in Hollywood—I think that it will have an important influence on his development. Have you seen his music? What do you think of it . . .?*

From Stravinsky to Nadia:

> *Boulez made an excellent impression on all of us: a musician of the very first rank, highly intelligent, he is well-mannered and is probably a generous man. His Marteau sans Maître, which he directed so well here, is an admirably organized score in spite of all its complications for both eye and ear (counterpoint, rhythm, measure). Without being familiar with this music of Boulez, I find it frankly preferable to a lot of things by his generation.*

From Nadia to Stravinsky:

> *I'm happy about what you say about Boulez—he's serious, he's a good musician—and there are no tricks, no bluffing. He was glad he saw you.*

It seems very apparent, however, that she was clinging to all this only with the tips of her fingers—those fingers which arthritis kept progressively warping to the point where, in 1954, she gave up playing in public. Holding steadfastly to an ethic which her adversaries considered to be irretrievably outmoded, she was afraid lest the musical world split into two camps incapable of reconciliation: she hedged, not wanting to find herself completely isolated.

This did not stop her from being ferocious after hearing certain works: "There is a category of people so afraid of letting a masterpiece slip by that they endorse everything: the less they understand, the more they wax enthusiastic. . . . There certainly do exist works we take for serious mental aberrations at the moment of their creation that turn out to be masterpieces, but I don't think that happens more than once in a century." And she added elsewhere: "There are a lot of musicians who, quite simply, cannot hear."

Besides, imperial and imperious as she was, what reason would she have had to doubt the soundness of her own judgment? Her fifty years of teaching, honored in 1954 by a big concert in Paris given by the Radio (which would bring out excerpts from the *Ville Morte* the following year) coincided with an unprecedented influx not only of Fontainebleau students but also of private pupils. She had a fanatically loyal following at the Conservatoire (clannish rivalries are always more radical at the

Crowding together during the Wednesday class at the rue Ballu

131

student level), and the rue Ballu was constantly buzzing with feverish activity. Agathe Rouart has described this atmosphere well: "United by their common zeal and by that irresistible authority which reduced them to total submission, her pupils came to her from all parts of the world, swarming into the rue Ballu salon, where the chairs were tight-packed between the organ and the two grand pianos with their great clutter of photographs, massive arrangements of azaleas and cyclamens, icons, and a great variety of objects bearing witness to Nadia's touching devotion to Lili . . . as well as to that of the faithful devotees of the *Boulangerie* to Nadia herself."

She made a triumphant lecture tour of Scandinavia, and was subsequently invited to Warsaw as a member of the competition jury, after having served in the same capacity in Brussels at Queen Elizabeth's composition competition. Finally, when the international Olympic committee wanted a hymn created for the 1955 Games at Melbourne, it was Nadia who was entrusted with arranging the contest, which offered a thousand dollar prize for three minutes of music.

She had the difficult task of getting a prestigious jury together in Monaco in April, 1955, at the request of Prince Rainier. Some of those whom she invited declined: Hindemith, for example; and she was especially hurt when Stravinsky also refused. He was in Europe at this time, but remained adamant, despite all the inducements she offered him, and despite her pleading—the word is not too strong. A Polish composer, Michal Spisak, carried off the victory over more than three hundred participants!

But above all else, when she was invited to the first International Festival of Contemporary Music, which took place in Warsaw in October 1956, she could not help but note with undeniable pride that most of the works presented were written by musicians who had passed through her hands. At this time she also had a brilliant group of Polish students, for whom she expended herself unstintingly, often with great selflessness, for she was aware that most of them were not in a position to take care of even the most modest expenses.

It is also worthy of note that most of her students, when they in turn became teachers, kept in close contact with her and came to see her regularly, even from great distances. As one of these students remarked, working with Nadia Boulanger left you with a life-long impression, perhaps less in your mode of musical expression which of necessity kept evolving, than in your innermost soul.

One of her American pupils, Don Campbell, accurately summed up what became the two aspects of her thinking: "Nadia Boulanger's words could on occasion be unique and profound. At other times they reflected the century in which she was born."

132

Her seventieth birthday, in September 1957, was celebrated at Villars-sur-Ollon, at the home of Igor and Topazia Markevitch: all her friends contributed to present her with a superb diamond. "Why not?" she had answered when they discreetly sounded her out beforehand, offering her a choice of gifts. The diamond, which she would wear in a pendant almost constantly from then on, was only one of many tributes. Her best friends had come, many of them from a great distance: Mr. and Mrs. Robert Woods Bliss were there, and all the Polignacs, including Marie-Blanche, for whom this would be one of her last social appearances. And Cuenod

Monaco in April, 1955, at the time of the Olympic hymn competition. From left to right: Georges Auric, Prince Pierre of Monaco, Nadia Boulanger, Kazim Aksès, Aaron Copland, Pablo Casals

133

and Conrad were there too, performing a mildly satirical little *Cantate N.B.*, composed for the occasion by Jean Françaix; and Poulenc sent a humorous "ode-minute." All this, together with the warmth of affection shown by her host and hostess, visibly moved Nadia . . . and compensated for the deeply felt absence of Stravinsky.

She had seen him again in Venice the year before, when she made a special trip there to attend the premiere of his *Canticum Sacrum* at San Marco, but the separation from him weighed upon her unbearably:

> *What wouldn't I give to be near you? . . . Seeing you is such great happiness— you bring so much to those who are drawn to you, and I . . . I love you so very much, just as much as I admire you. . . . One sometimes has a great need to say this, even while being quite aware of the uselessness of such effusions. But then, in the midst of the chaos with which musicians struggle, there you are, so great, so necessary, so right. . . . Come, come now, no more rhetoric!*
>
> *I send you a kiss: I'm dreaming of the moment when I will get to hear the music that is being created even as I write these paltry little lines. But they are, all the same, laden with affection and gratitude—and with everything that makes me your Nadia.*

These "effusions" constantly recur in her frequent letters to Stravinsky, along with the repeated expression of her "gratitude" for what he is, and for what he brings . . . So it is easy to realize how great her disappointment must have been a few years later.

In November, 1964, right after the death of Prince Pierre of Monaco, which she told him about, and which affected her deeply, Nadia asked Stravinsky to write a work for the following year in honor of the centennial of Princess Winnie. It was a commission from the Singer-Polignac Foundation, and she made it clear that "the sum involved might be ten thousand dollars." Three days later she received this telegram:

INFINITELY SORRY BUT THESE DAYS GET TEN THOUSAND DOLLARS TO DIRECT A CONCERT AND NOT LESS THAN TWENTY-FIVE THOUSAND FOR A COMMISSIONED SHORT PIECE THANK YOU VERY MUCH ALL THE SAME STOP HOW SAD TO LOSE PIERRE DE MONACO AFFECTIONATELY

IGOR

Nadia's seventy birthday candles illuminate Topazia Markevich under the amused eye of her husband

Stravinsky-the-man is completely revealed in this cruel, involuntary, five-line self-portrait. Without even considering friendship, how could he have forgotten everything he owed to these two women? Nadia played an important part in ensuring his welcome as a composer in his new country of adoption, where he had had difficulty establishing himself as a pianist. As for the Princess. . . . Would he have become what he was without her friendship, her influence, and her generosity, which remained unwavering for over thirty years?

Nadia, already depressed by the death of Pierre de Monaco, was wounded by this response. She admired the musician so much, however, that it did not occur to her to reject the man. Yet the tone of her letters reveals a sadness poorly hidden behind their conventional, sometimes ambiguous language. And at first she didn't even try to conceal her sorrow:

November 24, 1964

My friend,

Back home again—Monaco—days so heavy with sorrow, yet so luminous. I knew Pierre de Monaco very well and liked him very much—will the legacy he leaves behind somehow help us in the business of living, despite everything that departs with him?

I don't know whether you had the opportunity to find out who he actually was, so secretive, so alone, although so rich.

The Foundation was counting heavily on implementing this project, the only one that seemed the most beautiful to me, and the most right. . . .

On December 7, 1965, the concert took place in the salon with the black and gold frescoes by José-Maria Sert. The Singer-Polignac mansion was all lit up: a brilliant and elegant audience had come to pay tribute to the memory of a great lady. Nadia Boulanger directed a program of her own devising: works by Bach, by Schubert, and by Fauré alongside two of Stravinsky's recent compositions (how could one honor the memory of the Princess without thinking of Stravinsky? . . .), and Pierre Fresnay recited excerpts from Paul Valéry's *Cimetière marin.*

Nadia and Stravinsky wrote to each other less frequently after that, and circumstances were such that they were scarcely to see one another again. Their last meeting took place in 1968 in Paris, where Stravinsky had sworn never to conduct again " . . . after being insulted by both the public and the press at the premiere of my 'Threni' which I conducted myself at one of the Boulez concerts. And that's a final decision." At least, that's what he had told Nadia in 1967 when she had extended to him an invitation from André Malraux, who was at that time Minister of Cultural Affairs, to participate in the Baudelaire centennial ceremonies.

In Venice with Stravinsky, September 1958

The shock of Stravinsky's death in 1971 was somewhat attenuated for Nadia; now she was free to cherish without any reservation the memories she associated with the great non-serial works of this mighty genius, who became the little shopkeeper incarnate, perched behind his cash register.

One wonders when she found the time to think of herself or of her memories: never what one would call inactive, she kept on multiplying her activities as she advanced in age.

Although the guillotine-stroke of compulsory retirement at seventy had cut her off from her class at the Conservatoire in 1957, Cortot had asked her to come back that same year to the Ecole Normale, entrusting her with a class in harmony of which she would remain the titular head for twenty-two years, that is to say until her death.

In fact, a glance over this last period of Nadia Boulanger's life reveals an impressive diversity of activities as well as an extraordinary mobility at an age when people normally become more sedentary. She did not really stop traveling until she had reached her ninetieth year!

Her last trip, in the spring of 1976, was to Monaco, which had become, for her, a perennial symbol of all the good things that had come to her as a result of the active friendship of the Polignacs: from the time she was first appointed chapel-master in 1947, it had been her task to arrange the musical part of all the important ceremonies of the Principality, such as the funeral services of Prince Louis, and the coming to the throne of his grandson Prince Rainier in 1949, as well as the latter's marriage to Grace Kelly in 1956.

Like his father, the young monarch had a filial affection for Nadia Boulanger that dated from his childhood. An extensive correspondence covering a period of more than thirty years attests to the depth of his attachment, his admiration, his respect, his confidence, and makes clear how important it always was to him not only that she be welcomed and shown every attention, but that she approve of him.

The palace was always open to her. Nadia visited there many times, and was treated as one of the family by the princely couple and their children. On New Year's day, 1960, Prince Rainier wrote to her in his own hand, as was his wont:

> What a joy it is to have finally persuaded you to come to the Palace! You do know, dear Mademoiselle, that you are welcome to come whenever you wish, and to stay as long as you want to. Just let me know the day and the hour when you plan to arrive in Monaco—and by what means of transportation. I hope you will be kind enough and brave enough to talk to me about this musical composition competition.

Nothing in this world is perfect! And I can't claim to have produced anything perfect in my life . . . except for my two marvelous children! . . .

Well, one can always hope. Please be good enough to give me your opinion on the matter. We have to try . . . have to make an attempt . . . have to grope for the right way before doing well, or doing very well. So please be indulgent, for the best of intentions and enthusiasm have presided over the birth of this competition.

Nadia Boulanger, who was accustomed to demand things to be done, not just well, or even very well, but superlatively well, must have allowed herself to be convinced, since, from the following year onward, she was regularly a member of the competition jury.

Working with the brass section of the Hallé Orchestra

An orchestra rehearsal in Manchester, 1963

It is interesting to note that at the same time that Monaco was serving as a southern pole of Nadia's existence, it was being counter-balanced more or less symmetrically by a new pole in the north to which she was equally drawn. For in the English county of Surrey Yehudi Menuhin had at last created the school of which he had been dreaming for so long. There he welcomed gifted children attracted to music, undertaking not only their musical training but the whole of their education up to about the age of seventeen. It was not a school for virtuosos, but a nursery school to create good musicians with a solid foundation. Approximately thirty boys and girls from every corner of the planet, some of whom were very young, were brought together in a handsome red brick dwelling, in the midst of a park, to live the typical life of thousands of English schoolchildren, except for the fact that their masters often bore names that were famous in the world of music.

And so it was that Yehudi Menuhin had asked Nadia Boulanger, in the name of their long friendship, to supervise the overall organization of their musical studies. Nadia had known him thirty years earlier when he was not much older than the privileged children to whom he was now offering this rare experience; but since the war they had got together again, more or less on an equal footing.

Menuhin often appealed to Nadia, whom he deeply admired, to conduct concerts in the festivals he organized, in Gstaad as early as 1959, or at Bath, beginning the year after. She accepted this new task without hesitation, all the more eagerly because she had always felt that children ought to begin their musical education as early as possible. On the average of twice a year she spent several days at the "Ecole Menuhin," where each of her visits was an event of considerable importance.

It is remarkable that Nadia Boulanger, who terrified many of her adult students, generally won the affection of children. She intimidated them to some degree, of course, just as she intimidated everyone who came within her orbit, but they recognized in her, apart from a certain severity and a tendency to make awesome demands on them, that solidity they needed so badly—and which they are deprived of nowadays, in the name of relaxed standards. Nadia Boulanger's young pupils usually found the way to her heart, knowing as they intuitively did that even though she scolded them often, they could always count on her.

Surrounded by the children of the Menuhin School

141

England was the scene of many other of her activities. In addition to her involvement with the Menuhin School, she agreed to give regular master classes both at the Royal College of Music and at the Royal Academy of Music, the two great London conservatories.

And so, from 1960 to 1976, she made more than thirty trips across the Channel, dividing herself between her different professional posts, and at the same time performing on her own: doing broadcasts for the BBC, and making numerous public appearances, sometimes lecturing, sometimes conducting an orchestra.

In this respect the Anglo-Saxon countries offered her many more opportunities than her own country did: the English public especially, dazzled by the extraordinary renown that gave luster to her name, rushed to attend her concerts, some of which left a particularly strong impression. It sometimes happened, however, that the critics, though unanimous in praise for her ability to communicate her love for the music she performed, had some discreet reservations regarding her conducting abilities.

In America, she had been greeted with the same ardent enthusiasm on the one hand and mild criticism on the other. In 1958, between a tour of Denmark and a trip to Bucharest—where she served on the jury of the first Enesco Competition—followed by a stay in Venice, a stopover in Athens, and a brief sojourn in Turkey (where she gave a concert with Idil Biret, a pupil of whom she was very fond), she finally returned to the United States for the first time since the end of the war. She stayed two and a half months, from April 1 to June 14, ploughing a deep furrow all along the East coast, giving concerts, lectures, and lessons and classes in a number of prestigious universities.

It was almost a repeat performance of her major pre-war tours, though without her vocal group. There had been many changes in the interim, especially since her return to Europe twelve years before (Walter Damrosch had died in 1950, and a whole era had passed away along with him). But everywhere she was welcomed and applauded with the same enthusiasm mixed with admiration and respect, that is to say with the sort of veneration that gives rise to all manner of devotion. And Nadia Boulanger never ceased to demonstrate her unusual ability to dominate others, giving rise to attachments that at times bordered on voluntary servitude. At such times, she herself would allude to her "victims." The fascination she exercised and the lively response it elicited were in no way diminished by the passage of time. Nor did the passage of time in any way affect—at least in the United States—the preeminence of her "school." Even though in France she had to meet the challenge of ever-increasing competition, in America she was still considered to be without a peer.

The Bath Festival: Nadia and Yehudi during a break

Being prepared for a television film in Pittsburgh, 1958

At Fontainebleau, where she settled for the summer after her return from New York, a flood of students continued to pour in; with rare exceptions, they regarded "Mademoiselle" as a person to be revered.

One could almost feel her formidable presence behind each wall of the old Palace. Moreover, she initiated programs and meetings of which her students were the privileged beneficiaries: how rich was the list of artists whom they could approach and from whom they received instruction, if only by example!

It is not possible to mention all of them, but over the course of those brilliant years students at Fontainebleau had the opportunity to see and hear composers like Stravinsky, Poulenc, Copland, Dutilleux, Françaix; pianists like Clifford Curzon, Samson François, Arthur Rubinstein, Nikita Magaloff, Sviatoslav Richter, Robert, Jean, and Gaby Casadesus; violinists like Menuhin, Szering, Francescatti; cellists like Tortelier or Gendron; organists such as Marcel Dupré and André Marchal; and the singers Pierre Bernac, Denise Duval, Jessye Norman, Gérard Souzay; harpsichordists of the quality of Kirkpatrick and Puyana; the guitarist Narcisso Yepès; and in addition lecturers such as André Maurois, Serge Lifar, or Nicolas Nabokov. . . .

What an advertisement for Fontainebleau the prestige of Nadia Boulanger was. To say nothing of the young musicians to whom she gave a vote of confidence long before the public recognized their worth: Noël Lee, Régis Pasquier, Idil Biret (one of the triumphs of her teaching career), Miguel Estrella, the Fontanarosas, Pascal Rogé, Anne Queffelec. . . .

Master classes at Fontainebleau: Rubinstein, Enesco, Curzon

The traditional annual photograph at the Fontainebleau School, August 1963

147

In addition to working with the students at Fontainebleau, who often followed her to the rue Ballu after the two summer months at the School, she continued to maintain close ties with America. She never let much time elapse without returning there, after preparing her program very carefully. On December 22, 1960, Leonard Bernstein wrote to her from New York, where he was the musical director of the Philharmonic Orchestra:

> *My dearly beloved Nadia:*
>
> *I am so happy that you have accepted our invitation! Not only will your visit give great musical joy to a large public, but enormous personal joy to all of us who for so long have regarded you as the unique and adorable person you are.*
>
> *Don't you think it would be marvelous to play something of one or two of your former pupils?*
>
> *I look forward to seeing you with keen anticipation; and I was deeply moved by your beautiful letter.*
>
>

Always,

Lenny (Bernstein)
>
>
> *Joyeux Noël!*

Thirteen months later, in February 1962, at the head of the New York Philharmonic Orchestra, Nadia Boulanger would once again play Fauré's *Requiem* (she directed it some sixty times), *A Solemn Music* by Virgil Thomson, and the *Psaumes* by Lili Boulanger.

Four concerts in four days, each time to a full house: those who heard these performances of the Fauré *Requiem* remembered the interpretation as unequaled.

Nadia Boulanger had arrived a week before the first of these concerts, to a welcoming fanfare, since she had travelled on the *France* which was making her inaugural crossing!

She stayed for almost three months, spending time in Cleveland, in Chicago, in New Haven, in Boston (where she directed Fauré's *Requiem* once again) and in Washington. There, in the nation's capital, she was invited to lunch at the White House by John and Jackie Kennedy: her taste for celebrities made this occasion particularly pleasing to her. But it was while she was on this trip that she learned of the death of Tasha, a favorite cat, and an important member of the universe at rue Ballu and at Fontainebleau as well: "a very sad event," she jotted down in the little notebook in which only matters of major importance were recorded.

That was her last long stay in the United States, and perhaps the most triumphantly successful. She returned once more in 1965, but for only four weeks,

205 w. 57ᵗʰ St.
New York 19

My dearly beloved Nadia:

I am so happy that you have accepted our invitation! Not only will your visit give great musical joy to a large public, but enormous personal joy to all of us who for so long have regarded you as the unique and adorable person you are.

Don't you think it would be marvelous to play something of one or two of your former pupils?

I look forward to seeing you with keen anticipation; and I was deeply moved by your beautiful letter.

Always,
Lenny (Bernstein)
22 Dec 1960

Joyeux Noël!

Letter from Leonard Bernstein

which she divided between New York, Washington, Toronto, and Potsdam, where she signed a contract to give a six week course at the University the following year.

That was the engagement she broke at the very last moment, and for the first time in her life. She went instead to London where Hélène Détroyat (the granddaughter of her godfather, William Bouwens) had died suddenly. This cancellation was a great disappointment to the students from several states who had enrolled in large numbers in her classes.

She never went back to America again. But that same year, 1966, she had been invited to Moscow to sit on the jury of the Tchaikowsky Concours: it was not her first time in an "Eastern country" (she had been to Warsaw, and had on several occasions gone to Bucharest for the Liszt-Bartok Concours) but it was the first time she had returned to Russia, and to Moscow in particular, since the dramatic trip with Raoul Pugno, fifty-two years earlier. And that was before the coming into power of the Soviet regime, which she abhorred!

But the welcome they accorded her, and their rigorous fashion of teaching music, not unlike her own, made an impression on her, into which were mixed memories of her Russian mother and of her own origin: in her temperament there was a trace of the Russian noble.

New York, 1962: after one of the concerts, with Aaron Copland, Virgil Thomson, and Walter Piston (Billboard opposite)

New York Philharmonic
Music Director LEONARD BERNSTEIN
Thurs. Eve. Feb. 15 8:30
Fri. Aft. Feb. 16 2:15
Sat. Eve. Feb. 17 8:30
Sun. Aft. Feb. 18 3:00
NADIA BOULANGER
Conductor
RERI GRIST, MARGUERITE PAQUET
ROBERT ECKERT, DONALD GRAMM
VERNON de TAR, Organist
William Jonson, Director
FAURE Requiem Mass
THOMSON A Solemn Music
LILI BOULANGER Psalms 130, 129, 24
Columbia Records
Steinway Piano
PHILHARMONIC, 111 W. 57th St., New York 19
Moseley, Managing Director
William L. Weissel, Assistant
SOLD OUT

She still had a few fragments of Russian left over from childhood, but it was French and especially English that enabled her to converse. She struck up an acquaintance with the composer Kabalevsky, the very official secretary of the composers' Union of the USSR, and there was something more than a little paradoxical about the friendship that linked this devout Catholic woman whose politics leaned so far to the right a to be quasi-feudal to the atheist representative of an extreme-left regime—basically totally feudal!

It is true that Nadia Boulanger would have liked to believe in a common language linking all beings through music . . . but at the same time she kept making remarks which would have given her hosts ulcers, at least if they followed the official party line: "It's useless to try to give culture to the masses—to those who are not ready to welcome it."

Her last trip beyond the iron curtain was made the following year, on the occasion of the fourth Georges Enesco Concours: 1967, the year Nadia Boulanger reached eighty.

Prince Rainier wanted to have a memorable birthday celebration for her: he had been planning it for several years, unbeknownst to Nadia, but with the complicity of Annette Dieudonné, Doda Conrad, Igor Markevitch, Yehudi Menuhin, and a few others.

Moscow, 1966 during the Tchaikovsky Competition: above, in conversation with Emile Gilels; opposite, taking a walk with Dimitri Kabalevsky

Monaco celebrates the eightieth birthday of Nadia Boulanger; the arrival of Prince Rainier at the Monte Carlo Opera; at the palace with Princess Grace

It was a complete success, and the secret was at least partially kept: when Nadia arrived at the Monte Carlo Opera and was welcomed by Prince Rainier, the whole house stood up and gave her a long ovation. She was very touched by it, as she was by all the other displays of esteem that surrounded this event: Louise de Vilmorin had written a "congratulation" for her, which Markevitch's young son, Oleg, recited in the course of a concert on the program of which was printed a "homage" by Saint-John Perse, and an illustration by Chagall (Nadia was, of course, given the originals). The program included works by Bach, Monteverdi, Mozart, Fauré, and

Jean Françaix, interpreted by the orchestra of the Monte Carlo Opera, conducted by Igor Markevitch; also performing were Yehudi Menuhin, Mattiwilda Dobbs, Oralia Domingues, and Eric Tappy.

A more intimate dinner for forty guests was given in her honor by Prince Rainier and Princess Grace the following day at the Palace. After dinner, Nadia Boulanger received from the hands of Igor Markevitch the insignia of Commander of the Legion of Honor. (It was subsequently discovered that Markevitch did not have the requisite qualifications, so the ceremony had to be repeated some time later in Paris!)

Nadia withstood all this emotion and fatigue with remarkable stamina. But all the same she was beginning to show her age. It would have been reasonable for her to slacken the pace of her activities, but she was not at all willing to listen to reason, although at times she had no choice but to give in. For example, three years earlier she had had a car accident which might have been very serious, but from which she came away practically unscathed, as did Annette Dieudonné, who was with her at the time. The possibility exists that she fell asleep at the wheel, or perhaps her vision, which was progressively deteriorating, had played tricks on her. For once, she admitted that it was time to call a halt: at the age of seventy-seven she gave up driving, allocating the task to Giuseppe who became more and more a general factotum.

She was quite aware, also, that she ought to have an eye operation to arrest the deterioration and restore better vision, but she never had the time to attend to it, or didn't want to find time. It is true that, toward the end of 1967 and at the beginning of the following year, she was busy directing the recording of Lili's works. The fiftieth anniversary of Lili's death was commemorated by an exposition at the Bibliothèque Nationale. It was subsequently shown in Belgium and later in England, two countries where Nadia Boulanger on this occasion gave several series of concerts—between other tours in Switzerland and Portugal.

In 1969, she added Spain to the list of countries to which she went to give lectures and concerts, and she returned once more to Leeds where she served on the competition jury as she had done three years before.

In Paris her daily schedule was not at all that of a woman past eighty: even though the number of her pupils had diminished, it was still not unusual for her to give lessons hour after hour without the slightest interruption from nine in the morning to nine at night.

This pace was not without serious consequences, especially for her eyes: for all practical purposes she could no longer read; and she no longer wrote, dictating her daily correspondence instead.

At the Singer-Polignac Foundation in Paris, 1975: between Nadia Boulanger and Sviatoslav Richter is little Emile Naoumoff

After continuing to procrastinate for several more months, she finally gave in to the increasingly insistent urging of Prince Rainier, who finally took matters in his own hands: on February 12, 1971, she underwent a cataract operation in Monaco. It was completely successful, and would doubtless have had long-lasting good effect, if she had not resumed the bulk of her activities too soon: on March 5 she returned to Paris by the night train and met her one o'clock class the following day!

And, of course, she was back at Fontainebleau in July: they were celebrating the fiftieth anniversary of the founding of the American School, and she realized, sadly, that she was the last survivor of the epoch. But surprisingly enough she continued looking toward the future, thanks to the young people who still clustered about her as before. Especially close to her was a little nine-year-old boy from Sofia, whom his parents had entrusted to her a few months before–Emile Naoumoff.

From then on he practically never left her side; he was a constant joy to her during the nine short years that remained of her life. Although she never actually abandoned her proverbial severity nor relaxed her exacting pedagogical demands, she was, all the same, more indulgent in his case than she had ever shown herself to be before. She grew deeply fond of this child, of whom she wrote "the work accomplished always far exceeds in quantity and quality anything one could have hoped for." For his part, Emile was keenly aware of all that this woman, so close to the end of her life, offered him. They shared a deep mutual affection and understanding, and also a sense of gratitude that grew stronger with the passage of the years. Emile Naoumoff became, in a way, the living legacy of Nadia Boulanger. . . .

During one of her last visits to England, in lively discussion with Sir Arthur Bliss. Beside her are Zoltán Kodály and Ursula Vaughan Williams

In spite of her stubbornness, which far exceeded the usual norms, her physical resistance continued to decline. She put up a valiant struggle, with that energy always so characteristic of her, refusing to feel sorry for herself, and not tolerating the slightest sign of commiseration from others.

In June, 1972, she agreed to attend the inauguration of Place Lili Boulanger at Gargenville, to which, oddly enough, she had never wanted to return after the war. But the time came when she was obliged to lay down her arms, as, for instance, when she had to forego serving on the jury of the Rubinstein Competition in Jerusalem in 1973: long sojourns away from home were from then on out of the question for her, all the more so because she always refused to travel by plane; it was said that she made a solemn promise long ago to her mother to this effect. . . .

More and more it fell to Annette Dieudonné to shoulder the responsibilities of the Boulanger organization; in 1970 she was joined by another former pupil, Cécile Armagnac. Once again Agathe Rouart has vividly evoked the whirlwind atmosphere around Nadia Boulanger and "the imperturbable behavior of her acolytes, who were almost saints!—Annette and Cécile—and the Italian couple, so necessary to the functioning, the peace, and almost to the daily survival of that lively hive of activity in which were harmoniously blended toil and success, rigid discipline and broad under-standing . . ."

As long as she had the strength to do so, she forced herself to go to England to attend to her courses and, in 1975, she once again gave lectures at Cambridge, as well as at Zurich, and at Winterthur: her speech had become slightly sibilant, her delivery was slow, and her general intonation betrayed age and weariness, but her mind remained remarkably clear, without the least lapse from coherence in expression.

In March, 1976, she returned to London once again to hold her class at the Royal Academy, going from there to her children at the Menuhin School: it was to be her last visit. Two months later, she was in Monaco again, but there too it would be for the last time. From then on she left Paris only for Fontainebleau: in 1976, the artists whom she invited were Gérard Souzay, Clifford Curzon, and André Marchal—who was eighty-two years old himself.

It grew more and more difficult for her to make her body respond to her commands, but her mind remained keen-edged, clear, and broad-ranging, and her repartee lost nothing of its relevance, as is attested by the diverse interviews she granted at this time, especially those she authorized Bruno Monsaingeon to record in a number of sessions spread out over the last years of her life.

On February 9, 1977 at the Elysée Palace, the president of the Republic, M. Valéry Giscard d'Estaing, made Nadia Boulanger a Grand Officer of the Legion of Honor

It was during the first six months of 1976 that Nadia Boulanger allowed herself to be questioned, and even filmed, during some dozen afternoon interviews at the rue Ballu apartment. It is perhaps regrettable that these conversational interchanges did not take place earlier: but it is quite possible that, at any earlier time, she would have categorically refused to hold them since she never had the time to spare. Perhaps, also, she may have felt that, before it was too late, she needed to take inventory, and leave behind a testimony that would remain forever alive.

And what an astonishing inventory it turned out to be, when she was heard to say over and over again: "My life has been spent teaching." And what a teacher she was indeed! But had she quite forgotten those three thousand or so concerts she gave? Of course not, but she made this telling comment about them: "I have conducted. . . . That was the one luxury of my life." It was a luxury in which she could no longer indulge; as for Nadia the performer and Nadia the composer, they were not important in her eyes.

She fell seriously ill at the end of 1976, recovering just in time to attend a brief and cold ceremony at the Elysée, in which the president of the Republic, M. Giscard d'Estaing, made her a Grand Officer of the Legion of Honor on February 9, 1977.

This distinction, extremely rare for a woman, bore witness to the fact that her country recognized in her the exceptionally brilliant ambassadress of goodwill that she had always been. The recognition was also the symbol of the many honors that poured in upon her from everywhere over the course of a very few months, whether it was the Order of the British Empire, the Médaille d'Or of the Académie des Beaux-Arts, or the Médaille de Vermeil of the Ville de Paris, each of which occasioned receptions that, despite their formality, were very moving. From that figure slumped in the wheelchair, from that dark form with distant glance and heavy-bending head and snowy helmet of white hair, there still emanated a radiance all the more brilliant because one felt the flame was soon to flicker out. And indeed her failing health obliged her more and more often to cancel the few lessons she still gave; and the deterioration of her sight was now beyond repair.

At Fontainebleau, where Annette Dieudonné took her place in the classroom with increasing frequency, they celebrated her ninetieth birthday in advance on August 13, 1977. Emile Naoumoff, now fifteen years old, composed a piece for piano and violin as a surprise for her, and the young pupils of the Menuhin School came over especially to offer her a serenade. This warmly festive day-long celebration, which for Nadia's faithful followers had a hidden melancholy, wound up with the releasing of a host of tricolored balloons, after which, as night fell, the carp pool beneath the windows of Nadia Boulanger's apartment was brilliantly illuminated with lights which she could no longer see.

Everyone was fully aware of her extreme fragility, and felt a sad concern for the fate of the School, which had become in large measure "her" School. Would it ever open its door again?

In July, 1978, the doors did indeed open, and Nadia Boulanger was present in her accustomed place in her apartment in the Palace, which had been lovingly prepared in anticipation of her arrival. It was now quite out of the question for her to conduct her own classes: the task devolved upon Annette Dieudonné and Louise Talma.

In the beginning of the month of August, in critical condition, she had to be rushed to the Polyclinique; it was feared she was dying. But her formidable vitality enabled her to rally once again. She was, however, still very weak, and when she returned to Paris she slackened her pace for a while; in November she nonetheless resumed activity. Installed in her wheelchair, emaciated, and plunged in the night of her failed vision, she conducted her famous "Wednesdays," sad replicas of what they once had been.

But her mind was active, and she was still busy getting Lili's works republished, partly at Durand's, and partly at Schirmer's in New York: the final contracts were signed at the beginning of 1979. It was a great comfort to her to have been able to successfully accomplish this task, so dear to her heart; till the very end of her life, Lili continued to be an essential symbol for her. In spite of her state of exhaustion, she had herself taken to the Trinity Church on March 15, 1979, so that she might be present, crumpled in her chair, at the mass in which her sister and mother were united in her memory.

She knew that her hour was near, but she never entertained the thought of not continuing to struggle until her very last breath. In the month of April she consented again to grant an interview to a journalist, in between a few lessons which she gave in very small doses when her strength permitted. Her pupils—that is to say, their youth—were indispensable to her: "I love my pupils, I love to teach . . . I get a tremendous, crazy pleasure out of teaching. You have to hear and understand, and lead others to express themselves," she told him, making, as it were, a touching profession of faith.

To everyone's stupefaction, she insisted on being taken to Fontainebleau! She was still its titular head: her presence, even though unseen, would maintain the fiction.

Leonard Bernstein at the rue Ballu in 1978

When her familiar things had been sent on before her, she was taken there by ambulance on June 16. On the twenty-eighth, the students arrived in turn; a few carefully selected ones were allowed to go up to bow to her: seated in her armchair, her eyes lost behind thick glasses, she did not speak. . . .

She passed the month of July in a sort of lethargy, with only brief moments of alertness.

On August 10, an attack of fever threatened her life again. But the next day she felt better, and the day after, some of her students came to sing for her: Schubert (one of her absolute passions), Schumann, and Mozart. She was totally alert, and murmured in thanks: "I have enjoyed a moment of eternity."

She did not leave her bed again. No one was admitted. She was in physical distress; she had to fight for breath; attacks of fever made her delirious.

On the eve of their departure, at the end of August, her pupils came for the last time into her sitting-room to sing Mozart's *Ave Verum*, and a Bach chorale: the door stood open to the bedroom where she lay dying, emaciated, barely conscious;—one of those very close to her witnessed an "almost unbearable emotion."

Now the School was empty; no noise was to be heard in the vast corridors; the stone staircases were deserted. But its directress lived on there for another month, surrounded by her faithful ones, with Annette Dieudonné foremost among them.

On September 16, the day when she began her ninety-third year, Leonard Bernstein came to visit her from Paris, where he was passing through: he was not even sure that he would be allowed to see her. But in a flash of lucidity, she recognized him, heard what he said, spoke a few words to him, clung to him. . . .

He was one of the last to see her. It was no longer possible for her to take nourishment, and days without hope succeeded one another, ever growing darker; but she did not seem to be distressed.

Despite the misgivings of her doctors, the decision was made to take her back to Paris: summer was over, and the old Palace was cold.

The ambulance was ordered for October 5. Then began the dismantling of all those familiar objects which, summer after summer for the past thirty years, had made this setting seem like home to her: "Horrible melancholy of this departure from which there would be no return . . ."

In the now oppressive atmosphere of the museum-like apartment of the rue Ballu the body continued to struggle after the mind had fled, not giving in until Monday, October 22. In the early hours of the morning, she passed away in that same room where, seventy-five years earlier, she had fallen asleep for the first time beside Lili and her mother.

"Mademoiselle is no more," the newspaper headline read.

1904-1979, three-quarters of a century: Nadia Boulanger had just closed one volume in the history of music.

Paris, November 20, 1986

Acknowledgments

I heartily thank Annette Dieudonné, whose trust enabled me to produce this book.

Many others also provided valuable assistance to me: Miss Cécile Armagnac (particularly through the numerous documents she lent me); Mr. François Lesure, Head of the Music Department at the Bibliothèque Nationale, who granted special facilities to me; both the Fondation Paul Sacher in Basel and the Fondation Singer-Polignac in Paris where I received a friendly welcome; and the many personal testimonies I was able to gather, allowing me to refine this portrait of Nadia Boulanger.

To all of these friends and associates I wish to express my deepest gratitude.

J.S.

Bibliography

Campbell, Don G. *Master Teacher: Nadia Boulanger* (Washington: The Pastoral Press, 1984).

Cossart, Michael de. *The Food of Love: Princess Edmond de Polignac and Her Salon* (London: Hamish Hamilton, 1978).

Kendall, Alan. *The Tender Tyrant—Nadia Boulanger: A Life Devoted to Music* (London: Macdonald and Janes, 1976).

Lesure, François. "A travers la correspondance de Nadia Boulanger," *Revue de la Bibliothèque Nationale* (Paris: September, 1982).

"Lili et Nadia Boulanger," *La Revue Musicale* [double edition No. 353/354] (Paris: 1982).

Mademoiselle, a film by Bruno Monsaingeon [1973–1977]. Video cassette. (Paris: Editions du Lénard, 56bis, rue du Louvre).

Monsaingeon, Bruno. *Mademoiselle: Entretiens avec Nadia Boulanger* (Paris: Van de Velde, 1981).

Spycket, Jérôme. *Un diable de musicien: Hugues Cuenod* (Lausanne: Payot, 1979).

List of Illustrations

LIST OF ILLUSTRATIONS

Photographic Credits

All of the photographic documents reproduced in this book were kindly given to the author by the following sources: the Fondation Internationale Nadia et Lili Boulanger, the Bibliothèque Nationale, and the Fondation Paul Sacher. I offer my most sincere thanks to these generous institutions.

The plates included are to be credited to the following photographers:

Erich Auerbach, London
BBC, London
Freddy Bertrand, Geneva
The Boston Post, Boston MA
The Chronicle Library, San Francisco CA
Detaille, Monte-Carlo
G. Esparcieux, Fountainebleau
David Farell, London
Femina, Paris
France-Presse, Paris
Franck (Chalot & Cie), Paris
Studio Harcourt, Paris
Philippe Hutin, Paris
Keystone, London
Kollar, Paris
Victor Kraft, Paris
Lipnitzki, Paris

Photo Lukomski, Monte-Carlo
G. L. Manuel, Paris
L. Matthès, Paris
Nadar, Paris
Studio Piaz, Paris
Roger Picard, Radio-France, Paris
Studio Pierre Petit, Paris
Fred Plaut, New York NY
Axel Poignant, London
John B. Sanroma, Boston MA
Service photographique de la Présidence
    de la République française, Paris
Ben Spiegel, Pittsburgh PA
Studio Théo, Paris
Time Life, New York NY
The Times, London

Index